ARCHITECTURE FOR A CHANGING WORLD

ARCHITECTURE FOR A CHANGING WORLD

Edited by James Steele

■ THE AGA KHAN AWARD FOR ARCHITECTURE
▲▪ ACADEMY EDITIONS

ACKNOWLEDGEMENTS

This volume represents a close collaborative effort between the Aga Khan Award for Architecture and Academy Editions. I would particularly like to thank the Publisher, Andreas Papadakis, who has made this project a reality, and each of the individual members of the Award Steering Committee and Master Jury for their valuable advice, as well as Drs Yildirim Yavuz, Jamel Akbar, and Darab Diba of the Technical Review who provided essential information and help. I would like to extend gratitude to Nicholas Bulloch and Hasan-Uddin Khan and Van Nguyen-Lam of the Aga Khan Trust for Culture. For their continual support during preparation and production, I am grateful to Dr Suha Özkan, Jack Kennedy, Farrokh Derakhshani, Nabil Cherouati and Richard McAllister of the Aga Khan Award for Architecture.

Like so many others in the field of architecture, I would like to make special acknowledgment of the efforts of His Highness The Aga Khan, whose interest, enthusiasm, and generosity have so profoundly benefited the practice and study of architecture today.
JS

First published in Great Britain in 1992 by
ACADEMY EDITIONS
An imprint of the Academy Group Ltd.,
42 Leinster Gardens London W2 3AN

ISBN: 1 85490 173 7

Distributed to the trade in the
United States of America by
ST. MARTIN'S PRESS,
175 Fifth Avenue, New York, NY 10010

Copyright © 1992 The Aga Khan Award
for Architecture and Academy Editions

Printed and bound in Singapore

CONTENTS

Quality in the Built Environment and the Third World Reality *8*
Suha Özkan

Continuity, Relevance and Change
The Fifth Cycle of the Aga Khan Award for Architecture *14*
James Steele

A Pluralist Alternative *36*
Suha Özkan

Architectural Alternatives in Deteriorating Societies *40*
Mohammed Arkoun

A Tribute to Hassan Fathy *50*
James Steele

Contemporaneity in the City *53*
Hassan Fathy

The Search for a Socially-Responsive Architecture *60*
Arif Hasan

Jury Report *64*

Project Descriptions
Charles Moore and Selma al-Radi

ENHANCING URBAN ENVIRONMENTS 66
Kairouan Conservation Programme, Kairouan, Tunisia *68*
Palace Parks Programme, Istanbul, Turkey *90*
Cultural Park for Children, Cairo, Egypt *104*
East Wahdat Upgrading Programme, Amman, Jordan *124*
Kampung Kali Cho-de, Yogyakarta, Indonesia *140*

GENERATING NEW ARCHITECTURAL LANGUAGES 154
Stone Building System, Dar'a Province, Syria *156*
Demir Holiday Village, Bodrum, Turkey *164*
Panafrican Institute for Development, Ouagadougou, Burkina Faso *180*
Entrepreneurship Development Institute of India, Ahmedabad, India *188*

The Significance of Samarkand *200*

Project Data 212

Suha Özkan
QUALITY IN THE BUILT ENVI-RONMENT AND THE THIRD WORLD REALITY

It was the novel vision of His Highness the Aga Khan to contribute to the quality of the built environment by recognizing the achievements of the institutions and individuals whose efforts deserved to be encouraged and brought to the attention of a wider public as possible solutions to the continuing deterioration of the built environment. An important decision was to situate this endeavour within the realm of the architectural profession. Thus began a reciprocal and symbiotic relationship between the architectural profession in the Muslim World and the Award for Architecture, which has been continuously enriched since 1977.

When the Aga Khan Award for Architecture was announced, the architectural profession and all aspects of the built environment were highly complex and polarised. On one extreme, the newly emerging priorities of oil-rich countries sought to provide the very best infrastructure and architecture for their expanding cities; and on the other, at the fringes of hope, hundreds of millions in cities in Asia and Africa sought basic rights of shelter and mere survival. At both extremes, architecture was seen as an obvious solution but its definition and scope were different, and required re-formulation.

"A Search for Excellence" and "Quality of the Built Environment" were key expressions that guided the establishment of the Award. A meticulous, thoroughly conceived structure was devised at the Award's inception and was based on universal principles. The members of the first Steering Committee were the foremost practitioners and experts in the related fields of architecture, and highly committed. They envisaged the Award as a solid institution capable of enduring the changes of time, and tailored its procedures to include a process of evaluation that would be informed, credible, and - most importantly - independent. Therefore, the institution could incorporate the views, and sometimes the controversies, of changing, cyclical judgments and temporal statements to which the various juries,

FROM ABOVE: The Kampung Improvement Programme, Jakarta; Sherefudin's White Mosque, Visoko, Bosnia, Architect: U. Zlatko

8

sovereign in their mandate, would contribute. The decisions of each jury are presented to the widest possible forum, in order to stimulate open, critical debate. Accordingly, jury members are selected with particular care in order to reflect the current thinking of architecture on a worldwide scale, as well as to ensure quality, concern, and effectiveness.

To facilitate and enhance this thinking and to reinforce the intellectual tenets of the Award, a series of seminars were organized to explore and voice opinions in an academic forum; collectively, these seminars were later described as the Award's "Space for Freedom". Seminars remained thematic, in order to enable pertinent issues to be addressed in a geographical and societal context.

In 1980, the first cycle Master Jury identified fifteen winning projects. Their decision was a breakthrough in the broadening of the boundaries of architecture which, at that time, was confined to a classical definition dating back to the Renaissance. Ideas and concerns such as the problems of poverty and the pressing reality of informal housing in big towns have always attracted the attention of architects, but never as part of professional discourse. These issues formed part of their humanitarian concerns as fragments of contemporary reality that disfigured the urban environment. Contextualism was a popular theme, but mostly as an elitist attitude seeking to re-instate the grandeur of the scarred urban fabric of European cities. Alternative technology was an emerging idea and concern, but was always kept aside as a marginal issue that did not enter into the mainstream of architectural discourse. The Kampung Improvement Programme in Jakarta, Indonesia, the Medical Centre in Mopti, Mali, and the Agricultural Training Centre in Dakar, Senegal, were three projects premiated - and proudly acclaimed as examples of excellence - that otherwise would have been overlooked.

In addition to these, the work of a master, Hassan Fathy, and of his pupil, the designer of Halawa House, Agamy, Egypt, showed the great potential of traditional architecture, design and building practices, and brought them to the fore of the international architectural discourse. Appreciation and acceptance of traditional building systems had previously been limited to the architectural research media, but had never been

ABOVE: The Medical Centre, Mopti, Mali; Halawa House, Agamy, Egypt; Hajj Terminal, Jeddah, Saudi Arabia, Architect: Skidmore, Owings, and Merrill

so forcefully and so visibly recognized as they were by the Award in 1980. Appreciation of the contemporary idioms of architecture was also sentient but was eclipsed by a strong message that came to be identified as new priorities for the architecture of Muslim societies.

The second Master Jury, in 1983, referred substantially to the precedent established in 1980, and maintained a similar discipline of thought. In doing so, they did not hesitate to strive towards a more encouraging message for contemporary expressions wherever they felt that such efforts were appropriate to the indigenous realities of particular regions. The "hi-tech", state of the art Hajj Terminal in Jeddah, Saudi Arabia, and the unprecedented, free expressionism of Sherefudin's White Mosque in Visoko, Bosnia, securely placed the jury's debate on the cutting edge of contemporaneity. Within the same spectrum of decisions, the jury recognized the traditional idiom in its most pure sense and authentic form by premiating the Great Mosque of Niono in Mali. The same jury also made strong allusions to expressions of traditional form meeting the contemporary reality, as in the Ramses Wissa Wassef Arts Centre in Cairo, Egypt, and the Çakirhan House in Akyaka, Turkey.

The deliberate decisions of the third jury, in 1986, were very strong and indicated a new commitment as two members of the jury made dissenting statements. The jury decried the ills of the Modern Movement and celebrated the achievements of popular culture, traditional building and relevant contemporaneity in an urban context. The Bhong Mosque in Bhong, Pakistan, is an expression of popular building form, the Yaama Mosque in Tahoua, Niger, is a manifestation of uninhibited expression of sculptural form, and the Social Security Complex in Istanbul, Turkey, is a mature example of contextual architecture thoughtfully sited in the old city of Istanbul; all were highlights of the much-debated decisions of the 1986 Master Jury. The jury did not reach unanimous agreement, and the dissenting views voiced equally strong counter arguments.

The 1989 jury encompassed the widest range of architectural approaches. Their decisions raised considerable interest, from the point of view of the scope of the societal aspects of architecture, as well as the span of technology - from the most

FROM ABOVE: Great Mosque of Niono, Mali, Architect: Lassiné Minta; Ramses Wissa Wassef Arts Centre, near Cairo, Egypt, Architect: Ramses Wissa Wassef; Nail Çakirhan House, Akyaka, Turkey, Architect: Nail Çakirhan

rudimentary to the most sophisticated. The Grameen Bank Housing in Bangladesh aimed to provide dependable shelter in cyclone-prone areas, and affordable housing through a credit mechanism that enabled access to the basics of intelligently designed house types. It was contrasted with a steel and glass cultural centre, the Arab World Institute in Paris, France, with fine finishes and totally mechanised building systems. By doing so, not only was good architectural quality redefined within particular contexts, but the reality of rural areas, where almost two-thirds of the Muslim World reside, was addressed, as was the present-day reality of Muslims living outside their home countries. The jury also pointed towards important new discoveries, such as the Hayy Assafarat Landscaping in Riyadh, Saudi Arabia, where the provision of greenery and vegetation in a desert climate was achieved with minimal or no irrigation.

All four juries in the past have recognized architectural quality and have presented a wide array of alternatives with which architects working in the Muslim world may enrich their thinking and design approaches. Most importantly, the collective juries have posed the critical re-questioning of design priorities in the light of a new architectural discourse which has been nurtured, developed and disseminated under the auspices of the Aga Khan Award for Architecture. Many of these projects soon met with world-wide acceptance and were acknowledged as valid solutions to problems of a similar nature. The Residence Andalous in Sousse, Tunisia, and Mughal Hotel in Agra, India, the Tanjong Jara Hotel in Kuala Trengganu, Malaysia, and the Courtyard Houses in Agadir, Morocco, are among the projects which have had a wide impact upon many architects world-wide.

This year, 1992, marks the fifth cycle of the Award, with forty-eight different solutions and the life work of Hassan Fathy and Rifat Chadirji having been recognized by previous Awards as exemplary achievements in the field of architecture. As a part of this cycle, the Award held two intellectual activities. One of these was a meeting in Geneva, when the Steering Committee had the opportunity to discuss the Award's endeavours with three distinguished participants, an eminent architect, a renowned critic and an influential publisher. Frank Gehry, Alan Colquhoun and

FROM ABOVE: Bhong Mosque, Bhong, Pakistan, Architect: Rais Ghazi Mohammad ; Yaama Mosque, Tahoua, Niger, Architect: Falké Barmou

Andreas Papadakis attended this meeting.

The second event was an international seminar entitled "Expressions of Islam in Buildings", which focused on places of piety and worship. The papers and discussions that resulted from this event were published early in 1991.

The present jury has made a particularly strong judgment which, we believe, will engage architectural thinking around the world.

First, they declare that historical edifices should not be regarded as isolated, individual elements. Instead, the jury insists that they should be placed in the context of historic and urban environments with contemporary functions that accommodate uses and perform services in order to enable their continued importance in the lives of the people and to sustain their existence. The Kairouan Conservation Programme in Kairouan, Tunisia and the Palace Parks Programme in Istanbul, Turkey are fine examples of this attitude.

Secondly, the 1992 jury brings the social concerns of previous juries to a new level, highly evident in the architectural and design input in the improvement of existing settlements. In doing so, the jury sends a strong signal that the Award premiates projects at a higher level than the basic provision of infrastructure. The East Wahdat Upgrading Programme in Amman, Jordan, and the Kampung Kali Cho-de in Yogyakarta, Indonesia, contain architectural components much stronger than any other similar projects premiated previously.

Thirdly, there is a strong expression of the importance of larger natural and urban environments. No single project premiated in this cycle is an isolated, individual achievement, pointing to a sense of urgency for architectural inventions that engage in a stronger dialogue with societal and natural contexts. The Cultural Park for Children in Cairo, Egypt, and the Demir Holiday Village in Bodrum, Turkey, respectively, are examples of contextual interaction with the urban and natural environments.

The use of appropriate technology has always been one of the major areas to be explored by the Award. The introduction of inappropriate, imported or imposed technology has been diagnosed as one of the major ills of contemporary developments in architecture which have contributed to the disfigurement of the built environment. Furthermore, the explicit economies of

ABOVE: Diplomatic Quarter Landscaping, Riyadh, Architects: Bodeker, Boyer, Wagenfeld; Residence Andalous, Sousse, Tunisia, Architect: Serge Santelli; Courtyard Houses, Agadir, Morocco, Architect: J.F. Zevaco

using local materials which are readily available and abundant has the tremendous potential of harmonising with the natural context. In this cycle, the Stone Building System in Dar´a Province, Syria, and the Panafrican Institute for Development in Ouagadougou, Burkina Faso, are two novel examples of the use of simple technological innovations to enable building with local resources. The Stone Building System in Syria not only allowed the construction of elementary schools at a very low cost, but also questioned the widely-employed, standard school projects which are more usual, regardless of the availability of materials, climate, and all other local conditions. The example of Burkina Faso is the result of the wish of a dedicated group to build a major campus with a single material and simple building technology. In a similar vein, the Entrepreneurship Development Institute in Ahmedabad, India, employs a simple brick load-bearing structural system with standard pre-cast elements to achieve indigenous expression with direct reference to context.

In addition to these strong, well-articulated messages, there is one underlying element which binds all the projects tightly together - the quality of architecture and design. Even in projects with primary social and economic concerns, the use of design skills and architectural know-how has been closely examined and scrutinised. The dominant message of the jury - with all its emphasis on the condition of mankind - by no means undermines the manifestation of architectural quality, which has always been the central theme of the Award: to recognize the quality of the built environment by the full and appropriate use of design and architectural skills.

The deliberations of the fifth Award Master Jury indicate exciting directions for the Award's pursuit of a balanced synthesis of the highly sophisticated and valid values of architectural experience and the realities of Muslim cultures in a process of social, economic and environmental change.

ABOVE: Mughal Hotel, Agra, India, Architect: Arcop; Tanjong Jara Beach Hotel, Architects: Wimberly, Whisenand, Allison, Tong and Goo

James Steele
CONTINUITY, RELEVANCE AND CHANGE
The Fifth Cycle of the Aga Khan Award for Architecture

The three years that have passed since the last Award Ceremony in Cairo have been filled with events of staggering historical significance, which have had a great impact on both the physical and mental map of the Muslim world. Change, and the rate of change, have continued to accelerate at an incredible speed, bringing about the "Future Shock" predicted by Alvin Toffler several decades ago, as well as the "Global Village" described by Marshall McLuan. Time and space, which have been consistently abbreviated by the ever accelerating pace of travel and electronic communications, have now taken on a different dimension, altering the popular concept of context from local to international references in all parts of the world. Several generations ago, it was not uncommon for someone living within a traditional community to remain there for a lifetime, and the supportive circle that shaped that life was made up of family and friends and familiar faces that gave certainty and stability to daily routine. Such communities today are becoming increasingly scarce, as they are uprooted by forces that are beyond their control.

Since its beginnings in 1977, the Aga Khan Award for Architecture has been in the forefront of recognizing the full impact of such change, particularly as it relates to Muslim societies. This has set it apart from other efforts at recognizing excellence in architectural achievement, since it has not only sought to increase public awareness of the importance of good design, but has gone on to designate the broader social and cultural aspects of architecture in regard to people, and not just professionals. It has emphasized the importance of an informed, interdisciplinary dialectic in trying to come to terms with the problems of the built environment, which has, until this current cycle, evolved into the recognition of projects as they relate to either socioeconomic, historic conservation, or the pursuit of architectural excellence. Behind this search, a constant concern has been to encourage unrestricted critical debate, which Mohammed Arkoun has analyzed as falling into three categories. The first of these, in his view, has been to seek out: "the historical objective knowledge of the classical legacy of what is called Islamic culture and civilization, or *turath* in Arabic; the idea is not to compete with the established scholarship in this field, but to reflect on the relevance, the meaning, and the results of the continuous reference made today to this classical legacy as the model for the contemporary expressions of "Islam" as a whole (religion, culture, civilization)."

The second concern, in his view, has been to identify: "the dominant forces, models, conceptions, achievements which are actually at work and are spread today throughout all Muslim societies and which are not related at all to the claimed ideal model; in other words, the built environment and the cultural expressions of "Islam" are subjected to an irresistible process of deterioration, disintegration, destruction."

And thirdly, as he has said, the Award has sought to help to identify: "new ways, new methodologies, new conceptions, new tools, to provide for an enabling culture and thought that would stop the process of rupture with the classical legacy, would help to recognize the living tradition, and, at the same time, would contribute to the invention of modernity in Muslim societies."[1]

In concluding his assessment of the importance of the Award, Arkoun has also said that:"This approach, including a long-term historical perspective and a free but critical acceptance of all the challenges of modernity, is probably unique as far as Muslim societies are concerned. It is not to be found in any known type of scholarship - Muslim or orientalist - in any tradition of teaching, in any private foundation or trend of thinking. That is why the Aga Khan Award for Architecture is so conscious of its responsibility and so eager to go further in the path successfully traced over a decade."[2]

As the Jury convened for the fifth cycle, there was a sense of urgency brought on by the magnitude and rapidity of current events, the need to consolidate what has already been established, and to redefine parameters for the future. Given the reshuffling of the world order that has now taken place, questions about how these changes will affect Muslim societies in the *next* fifteen years were a part of the unspoken agenda this past June in Geneva, as were the effects of such shifts on architectural, and particularly urban, expression.

The Pattern of Past Awards

In order to fully appreciate the full import of this change over the last three years, it may be helpful to review the three categories that had previously evolved as the main concerns of the Award, which had become the framework by which projects were selected, so that a comparison with the position taken by the Jury for this fifth cycle may be constructively drawn. In reflecting on the progress of the Award up to the time of the presentation ceremony at the Citadel, in Cairo, His Highness the Aga Khan noted that three strong themes of concern have emerged. These, as he said at the presentation ceremony, were:

"First: protection, restoration and the skilful re-use of the *heritage of the past*, at a time when that heritage, the anchor of our identity and a source of our inspiration, is being threatened with destruction by war and environmental degradation or by the inexorable demographic and economic pressures of exploding urban growth.

Second: addressing the pressing needs for *social development and community buildings* in a Muslim world all too beset by mass poverty.

Third: identifying *contemporary architectural expression* of quality, the best efforts at capturing the opportunities of the present and defining our dreams of tomorrow."[3]

Conservation

As the means by which the *turath* described by Mohammed Arkoun, as related to its tangible, architectural remains, may be perpetuated, conservation has been recognized as a valid area of concern for the Award, being divided between restoration projects (the Al-Aqsa Mosque, the Tomb of Shah Rukn-i-'Alam, and the Ali-Qapu, Chehel Sutun and Hasht Behesht), adaptive re-use projects (the Azem Palace, Rustem Pasa Caravanserai, National Museum in Doha, and Ertegun House in Bodrum), and area conservation projects (conservation of Mostar Old Town, the Darb Qirmiz Quarter in Cairo, and Sidi Bou Said in Tunisia). Conservation has taken on

added significance with the passing of time because as cities continue to develop at an alarming rate, causing dramatic demographic shifts from rural to urban areas and the concomitant fragmentation of traditional societies, and the *Waqfs* that have been responsible for the upkeep of major monuments continue to lose their ability to do so, the architectural heritage in all of the long-established cities of the Muslim world has continued to decay rapidly. Since much of this heritage has either fallen into disuse, or not been adapted to a new use that will continue to prolong its life, it has been especially vulnerable to the effects of this population shift, and many of these historical remains are now located in the poorest part of Muslim communities.

In Cairo, for instance, many of the oldest buildings in the medieval section of the city, which stand exposed and vacant because of the lack of resources, have become shelters for the rural poor who pour into the city every day, seeking a better life. In a majority of cases it is the only habitation they can find, or can afford, and in their extremity they inadvertently help to hasten destruction which has already been accelerated by water penetration that has caused bursting of wall surfaces due to the crystallisation and expansion of separating salts in the masonry, or vandalism and fires.

Because of their poor condition and the complexity of the social issues involved, these areas are frequently given low priority at a national level, but since the Award has begun to recognize conservation and restoration efforts, priorities have begun to change, and Muslims are now more aware of their cultural heritage and identity.

As they have evolved over the course of the last four Award cycles, three kinds of conservation efforts have been considered by the Master Jury. The first of these, which is conservation of a specific historic monument, takes into consideration its value over time and the extent to which the restoration effort has conformed with the standards established by the Venice Charter, including the concept of reversibility. In this category, the historical significance and aesthetic value of the monument are obviously of prime importance, but other criteria that have been taken into account are: the historical accuracy of the restoration, the level of scholarship involved, the perfection of the technical details and the quality of workmanship, and the appropriateness of the use of materials and methods. The degree to which new materials were used in the restoration, and their capacity to harm its basic structure or finish, are an important consideration in the determination of appropriateness. The use of local craftsmen and the degree to which the project revives traditional techniques are also important, since this has a direct impact on the extent to which local inhabitants are involved in the entire process, and encourages them to take pride in their own architectural heritage. The use of local craftsmen has an economic parameter also, since it reduces the cost of the project and makes the techniques that have been used more practical in their future application elsewhere.

The second category of consideration has been adaptive re-use, which involves the restoration of an old structure, and conversion from a previous to an appropriate new use. The success of applicability of the transformation, as well as the aesthetic quality, the technical difficulty involved in the adaptation, the quality of restoration work, and the materials used have all been taken into account in determining the appropriateness of the restoration. In this regard, it is interesting to note that not every historic building adapts well to re-use, as architect Aldo Rossi has indicated in his discussion of the role of the monument in the shaping of urban form in *Architecture of the City*. In defining the difference between those structures that do and those that do not, he has used the graphic terms "perpetuating" and "pathological" to show how adaptation can take place in some instances and is impossible in others, leaving the building in question as a lifeless artefact of another time.

The third category, area conservation and rehabilitation, is at the opposite end of the spectrum from the restoration of an individual building and recognizes the conservation of the built form of a complete traditional environment to be possible. The implications of a sensitive recognition of the viable interdependence of pre-existing neighbourhood patterns and the survival of built forms and open spaces on the reinvigoration of old urban areas and inner cities have been key elements in this category, which has the most important implications for the 1992 cycle. While the focus here is on the fabric as a whole, the conservation of individual monuments within it is

ABOVE: The Kairouan Conservation Programme has relied upon the symbolic power of important historical monuments to re-enliven the urban fabric; PAGE 14: The As Suwayda' Elementary School.

typically a critical ingredient as may be seen, for example, in Fatehpur Sikri or Isfahan. In this regard, the Award has sought to recognize projects that address large urban areas or rural settlements, in which the preservation effort has attempted to perpetuate overall character through a process of upgrading, restoring, or even restricting the construction of inappropriate new building styles and methods within their limits.

In one of a collection of papers prepared as a result of a workshop sponsored by the Aga Khan Trust for Culture, on Architectural and Urban Conservation in the Islamic World, held in Dhaka, Bangladesh in 1989, Sherban Cantacuzino has provided some additional thoughts which are extremely useful in establishing the extent of this category. In his view, these consist, first of all, in deciding on the criteria for listing buildings and designating conservation areas, and surveying both. Before doing so, he stresses that it is necessary to judge historical significance, stylistic integrity, uniformity of quality and social and economic use and viability. Secondly, area conservation consists of the listing of individual buildings or groups of buildings to ensure their preservation and protect their setting. Thirdly, in the designation of conservation areas, it is vital that such identification be recognized as a means by which their character and integrity may be enhanced and maintained. The implication of such a designation, as a fourth consideration, involves the design of controls and guidelines for the area, as well as the setting of social and financial incentives and the training of craftsmen. Fifth and last, is the establishment of mechanisms for operating the programme, including an advisory body within the civic or regional authority and the training of professionals for follow through. In putting forward these refinements, Cantacuzino makes a plea for the economic viability of such an approach, which is often dismissed as being beyond the financial means of many authorities. As he says: "In the Third World countries architectural conservation, in the sense of area conservation rather than monument conservation, is not usually high on the list of priorities, yet area conservation, far from being unaffordable, can actually save money by making sensible use of existing resources."[5]

Two projects chosen for awards in this fifth cycle are both representative of this wider, contextual approach, and would have logically fallen into this category as established in the past. They are, in an initial comparison, completely different in approach, and yet similar in the higher perspective that they share.

The Kairouan Conservation Programme, as first undertaken by the *Association pour la Sauvegarde de la Médina de Kairouan* in 1977, began as an initiative to safeguard the architectural, cultural and historical heritage of the entire *Medina*, to protect it from indiscriminate modernisation, and to contribute to the socio-economic revival of the whole town. As a model of the process that Cantacuzino describes, the project started with a careful assessment of the major monuments in the *Medina*, with the additional dimension of creative suggestions for their adaptive re-use contributing to its final success. While academic purists may quibble about these changes of function, they have allowed the larger monuments to recapture their original status as vital, recognizable landmarks in an otherwise homogeneous urban fabric, and to give them a new sense of purpose. Examples of these changes are: the Khan Barrouta built in the 18th century has been transformed into a crafts centre; the Bir Barrouta (a two-storey structure containing a water well dating from the early days of Kairouan but restored during the 17th century) has been made into a reservoir; three old suqs, including the suq of Cisterns (14th century) have been transformed into modern shops; the Mausoleum of Sidi Khedidi (18th century) has been converted into a special school for the deaf and dumb; the Mausoleum of Sidi Aloumi has been converted into a new social information office; the Sidi Abdelkader Mausoleum (19th century) has been put to use as a centre for diabetics; the Mausoleum of Sidi Siouni has been converted into offices for the Nature Protection Society; the Mausoleum of Sidi "Amor" Abada (19th Century) has been transformed into a Museum of Popular Arts.

All of these changes were preceded by a careful survey of the entire fabric, in which buildings were ranked so that resources could be directed more effectively; and in determining the position of each structure in this six-stage filter, its inter-relationship with neighbouring structures was also considered. Once the principal monuments were assessed, rehabilitation was carried out with due respect given to their historical significance. In addition to the immediate benefits this upgrading had for the local inhabitants, it also increased the number of tourists to the *Medina*, which raised the level of employment and income. This twofold visual and economic improvement encouraged citizens to participate even more in the rehabilitation programme, by contributing time, money, or both. Funds obtained from admission fees resulting from improvements to the major monuments have repeatedly been recycled back into helping upgrade the rest of the community, providing an inspiring example of what can be accomplished through modest means and clear, uncomplicated organization. By approaching the rehabilitation of the priceless architectural heritage of the *Medina* as an entity, rather than concentrating only on specific parts, the Kairouan project offers tangible proof of the benefits of taking an inspired overview of such problems.

In comparison, the Regional Offices of the National Palaces, which were entrusted with the administration of a series of Ottoman structures built over a period of two centuries starting in the early 18th century, including the palaces of Dolmabahçe, Beylerbeyi, and Yildiz, and the Pavilions of Aynalikavak, Ihlamur, and Maslak, were faced with the task of conserving the revitalising relatively isolated monuments linked only by their combined significance to Turkish history. As symbols of a time when cultural perceptions shifted from East to West, making a break with the attitudes represented by the Topkapi Sarai, these palaces and pavilions have now taken on an additional layer of meaning, considering the national preference for joining the EEC. Unlike the jewel-like focal points of the Kairouan *Medina*, these six projects have no residential fabric surrounding them, placing a different kind of responsibility on restorers to suggest an aura rather than actuality. In spite of the differences between the character of their context, however, the similarities between the two projects, in terms of the attitude taken by those responsible for them, are striking. The National Palaces Trust, like the *Association de Sauvegarde de la Médina de Kairouan*, has placed a high priority on research to be carried out before, during and after any restoration. The conservation and restoration section of the NPT is headed by the Director of

ABOVE: The skill of the stone mason has been a critical factor in the Palace Parks Programme in Istanbul.

Building and Garden Repairs who co-ordinates the activities of four architects and three engineers, as well as a team of scientists at the Central Conservation Research Laboratory based at the Dolmabahçe Palace complex. All decisions are taken on a case-by-case basis by the architectural and engineering staff in consultation with experts on the team. In future, collaboration with ICCROM is planned, and architects, stonemasons and fresco painters will be sent there for training in modern techniques. This programme depends heavily on independent, personal initiative unencumbered by strict organizational guidelines. An example of this is the discovery of a stone quarry near Istanbul that could supply limestone identical to that used in the palaces, and the recommendation to the Director by the site architect, who found it, that it be used. As the technical reviewer for this project said in her report: "Because the system is so dependent on the site architects, the benefits of any external technological advice given directly to the architect are immediate and obvious... The architects are gradually becoming more conscious of tradition in the process."[5]

The technical reviewer goes on to describe how the research laboratory and crafts workshops are set up, which is indicative of the level of care that is typical of the programme, noting that the craft workshops under the technical team include bookbinding, woodwork, stonework, upholstery, glasswork, lead sheet casting, and a locksmith. In some cases, craftsmen have been working in the palace for twenty years. The crafts workshops also have a training programme attached to them and there are forty to sixty students taken on each year from the technical schools for a period of two years training by the Dolmabahçe craftsmen. Each craftsman usually has two or three students working with him.

The research department, enlarged in 1984, is made up of six people with an equal number of assistants. During the past two years a research training programme has also been instituted. Nine researchers from different universities working on art and architecture of the 19th century have been recruited to work on the premises and continue their research under the guidance of the Director of Research of the NPT, but the post will soon become an official government position.

The research team has started to catalogue the objects in the palaces, and has developed a new computerised inventory system, based on that of the Topkapi Sarai. New archival material discovered in the Palace in 1985 is also in the process of being catalogued by the department. More detailed guides have been prepared and are due for publication soon. They have also begun to put together the archival material in different libraries and private collections, and are attempting to acquire copies of these.

A second similarity between the Palace Parks Programme and the Kairouan Medina project is the creativity used in converting each monument to a contemporary use. In the case of the Palaces, Dolmabahçe, as indicated, has become headquarters for all restoration efforts; while Beylerbeyi has been partially converted into a museum, with the extensive gardens and a video room proving to be especially popular. Aynalikavak, which is the oldest of the palaces, will also eventually become a museum, specializing in traditional Turkish musical instruments, which will tie into the proposed concerts to be held there. Maslak, which is located at the edge of a forest, is to become a sports campus, with recreational complexes amidst the trees, as well as exhibition spaces. Ihlamur has been rehabilitated in connection with a children's educational programme related to it with particular attention given to its beautiful gardens, and Yildiz Sale, which is mostly used as a museum, also includes an auditorium and cafe.

In its ambitious attempt to make a neglected part of the national heritage accessible to the public once again, the Trust has had to evolve an empirical system to achieve its aims and to perpetuate them. The lessons learned in this process are important for others who are also involved in architectural conservation in a growing metropolitan area. The success of this project lies in the ability of the organizers to look beyond obvious choices to the needs preference of society, in order to make learning about history less burdensome and more of a joy. As the technical reviewer said: "It must be recognized that the project is unique, in terms of scale, historic importance and governmental support. The work of the NPT is therefore commendable, exactly because of the scale of the project. Although the actual implementation of the conservation and restoration work varies, the overall

impact of the different projects is very positive. The combination of training with the revival of the palace crafts workshops is a feature worth praising. The success of activities for the local population, such as the children, is indicative of a social function fulfilled. The creation of research positions in another activity must be applauded for its foresight."[6]

In the same series of papers on restoration that produced Sherban Cantacuzino's expanded criteria for area conservation, Mohammed Arkoun has noted that, in the developing world, there are many demands on extremely limited resources and that these frequently exclude conservation from political consideration. He emphasizes the need to continue to recognize the kind of efforts represented by these two projects as a vital part of social and cultural development, and by bringing such considerations into the realm of popular participation, the Kairouan Conservation and Palace Parks Programmes have already begun to do just that.[7]

The Social Dimension

In regard to "Architecture for Societies", as defined by His Highness the Aga Khan in Cairo in 1989, the Award has typically seen it as being related to the vast majority of Muslims who live in poor countries with inadequate resource bases, low per-capita incomes, and high rates of population growth. Their governments characteristically do not have the financial, technical and managerial resources required to tackle the immense problems related to poverty and the environment. Additionally, government planning is usually based on conventional models adopted from the first world which, apart from being capital intensive, do not make use of the considerable skills, vitality, and ingenuity that poor communities possess. The cost of formal private sector development and services, on the other hand, is beyond the financial capacity of low income groups. Thus, an increasing majority of Muslim communities are being denied access to decent shelter, physical infrastructure, and social services, or are being serviced by an exploitative and technically defective informal sector.

A number of projects in the Muslim world, such as the two Kampung Improvement Programmes in Indonesia and the Grameen Bank Housing Programme in Bangladesh, which have been

ABOVE: The Grameen Bank Housing Programme, which received an award in the Fourth Cycle, has been an an inspirational example of the way that institutional attitudes can change.

recognized by the Award in the past, show that innovative approaches involving communities can make development compatible with the sociology, culture, and economic conditions of the poor and can affect their levels of awareness and living conditions in a positive fashion. If such programmes are replicable and sustainable, then they can be increased in scale in order to have a major impact on the larger social and physical environment.

It is undeniable that such schemes almost always lack the visual impact of individual buildings designed by architects for government clients or for more affluent sections of society. However, considering the scale, complexity, and seriousness of the problem, the Steering Committee has given considerable importance to such projects and feels that there is a great need to alert the architectural profession and academic institutions to the relevance and importance of work that can have a lasting impact on the lives of many. Consecutive Award Master Juries have endorsed and given impetus to this concern and have demonstrated that it would be inappropriate to focus on the architectural excellence of individual buildings without taking note of the expanding sea of human misery and degradation that often surrounds them. This has been the background of the 1992 cycle.

In assessing the social projects nominated for the Award, in the past the Steering Committee has stressed that the more important criteria, among others, are relevance of the project to the context of the country, its compatibility with the social and economic reality of the beneficiaries, its sustainability, its social and physical impact, and replicability. While replicability is fairly easy to determine the notion of sustainability is still a bit general, and requires elaboration. In many ways, the concept of sustainable development was a driving issue for the jury in this current cycle, due to the growing awareness of global interdependence, the environment, and population growth that has spawned the idea. The concept must then be seen, in each instance, within the much wider framework of such inter-relationships, so that its significance can be gauged more accurately. The critical linkage in this framework is the realization, which has just recently taken place on an international scale, that we are all responsible for the environment. The recent

Environmental Summit in Rio de Janeiro, Brazil, clearly demonstrated the extent of this awareness, as well as the complexity of the geo-political problems involved in reaching any consensus on the management of these resources. This attitude of "management" is also relatively new, and is indicative of a somewhat industrialized notion of the allotment of a specific commodity. Regardless of its materialistic viewpoint, the concept does serve as a useful way of helping many people to visualize the degradation of the environment. The idea of sustainability itself only dates from the mid-1980s, when it began to appear in research reports at the International Institute for Applied Systems Analysis in Austria, as well as those of the World Commission on Environment and Development. As subsequently refined by the WCED, sustainable development has been defined as "a path of social, economic and political progress that meets the needs of the present without compromising the ability of future generations to do so.[8] William Clark has since gone on to refine this definition by focusing on the aspect of equity that is implicit in it, and the notion of values, which differ from one society to another. The equation reducing the use of global resources to a ratio in which 15% of the earth's population has been consistently shown to use one third of them, while 25% of its people go hungry, is now common knowledge, as are population trends, which show that the doubling that will take place during the next hundred years will happen almost entirely in the developing world. As Clark, and many others trying to predict the consequences of such growth have made clear, a dramatic increase in economic productivity will be necessary in a very short period of time to even maintain basic levels of subsistence in most of the countries now categorized as "developing" and the impact on an already threatened environment could be "catastrophic."[9]

Facts such as this, however, which have already been subsumed into the collective consciousness, are only the beginning of the story, which, as it relates directly to the cultures represented by the awards described here, is far more convoluted and important to understand. Chris Abel, whose conclusive survey of regionalism in *Architectural Review* several years ago helped to lead the way toward such comprehension, has recently expanded on the thesis presented there with some interesting results.[10] Abel favours the concept of "ecodevelopment" over that of sustainability. In a recent paper entitled "Ecodevelopment: Toward a Development Paradigm for Regional Architecture" he begins by analyzing the dynamics of colonial imperatives, which provide a more realistic, historical background to the elemental imbalance that is operative today.[11] He argues that colonialism, rather than bringing the benefits of technology from their source to the countries that needed them most, as myth would have it, "actually meant a diversion of local energies away from those pursuits which were necessary for self-sufficiency, such as the growing of food supplies for local consumption, toward the mining and cultivation of resources for export to service the metropolitan economy."[12] The material inequity that now exists, which prognosticators predict will be redressed by natural forces of population growth and the economic exchange of the international market-place, and which now forces manufacturers to seek less expensive means of production, is not the consequence of systemic, cultural or geographic divisions. The replication of any models used to perpetuate such inequities, only serves to extend these differences. Those agencies which propose a wholesale importation of sophisticated technologies into areas that lack them, generally rationalize the interchange with the argument that such a transfer is necessary to establish equity, when it really only perpetuates dependency. As Abel notes, the futility of such logic, has led to "a number of "alternative" development strategies ... which challenge orthodox theory and practice. The most promising of these is ecodevelopment, a term coined by Maurice F. Strong, the first Director of the United Nations Environmental Programme and Director of the recent Earth Summit in Rio de Janiero. Ecodevelopment policy explicitly rejects the assumption that development should always be modelled on Western industrial patterns, or that such development should be concentrated in urban centres, or even that unfettered urbanization is a natural or desirable consequence of development."[13] He then goes on to refer to Strong's definition of ecodevelopment directly, which is based on the belief that it should occur at the regional and local level, and "should be consistent with the potential of the area involved; with attention given to the adequate and rational

ABOVE: The Rehabilitation of Asilah, also recognized in 1989, was a precursor of the category "Enhancement of the Urban Environment" recognized as being so important by the 1992 Master Jury.

use of national resources, and to appreciation of technological styles (innovation and assimilation) and organizational forms that respect the natural ecosystems and local socio-cultural patterns."[14]

In recalling and advocating social and economic patterns of the kind first popularized by E.F. Schumaker in *Small is Beautiful* two decades ago, Abel, through such references, also cautions against pre-emptory value judgements, and carefully examines the word "appropriate" in this context. When discussed in connection with technology, as it was initially by theorists such as Hassan Fathy, the term implied a *techne* modulated by the means and materials available to a particular people, place or region, and did not preclude acceptance of a sophisticated technology in a social system, and a naturally rich location that can justifiably support it. Abel reminds us that due to possible misunderstandings related to the word "appropriate", Schumaker proposed that "intermediate", be substituted instead, eventually establishing the Intermediate Technology Development Group to implement his ideas![15] Whatever label is given to them, such technologies, in Abel's view, "are designed to fill the gap between capital intensive and unsuitable imported technologies, and inexpensive but often inefficient traditional technologies. Typically, they are low in capital costs, use local materials whenever possible, are labour intensive, small scale, easily understood and easily produced by people without high levels of education, involve decentralized renewable resources ... and are flexible so that they can continue to be used or adapted to fit changing circumstances."[16]

The basic message which such debates convey is that, labels such as "sustainable" and "appropriate" have now taken on several layers of meaning, and must be carefully considered, in terms of intention and context. Given the global consequences involved in regional decisions, which now have ramifications that operate through an intricate network of dependent elements, terms must be weighed carefully, and used correctly. As the awards in this category have demonstrated in the past, there must also be a distinct differentiation made between self-help, without a concomitant, formally impressive architecture resulting from it in the typical sense, and an architecture that promotes self-improvement, dealing with latent talent, aspirations, the basic desire for

dignity, and the indomitable will to survive, which are the most valuable, and elusive human resources of all. In terms of self-help, housing remains the most accurate barometer of changing attitudes towards the role that governments and institutions should play in providing shelter, and this entire issue has been discussed at length at an International Seminar sponsored by the Aga Khan Award for Architecture, the African Union of Architects and the Association of Architects of Tanzania, held in Zanzibar in 1988. At the opening of that Seminar, His Highness the Aga Khan revealed the heart of this problem when he said that:

"In the seamless web we call national development, housing is only one factor influencing the quality of human life. But how vital it is to health and human safety; still more fundamentally, the state of a persons's home touches deep chords in the human spirit. It can make him proud or ashamed; give him light and a sense of hope or deepen his despair. It is his statement to his children and to the world about his control over his life, and his aspirations for the future. It is not too much to say that to the extent a man is a householder, he is also a citizen with a permanent interest in the stability and progress of his country. Still more important, housing has historically been created by families... It is into this deeply personal relationship between a human being, his family and neighbours, and his environment, that the state, with the best of intentions, has entered. Often it has little choice. The sheer magnitude of homeless thousands, has required large scale responses. Limitations of available capital, materials, management, and technical know-how seemed to dictate that governments adopt quick, low-cost solutions in the form of mass housing for low income groups. No wonder, given the size of the problem, governments have concentrated on bricks and mortar. But even when conceived by geniuses, these solutions have rarely been successful. Europe, North America, and the developing world all abound in failures, slum clearances and mass housing schemes that have not looked as human settlements, and have become instant slums and centres of despondency and crime. I deeply believe that the developing world is entering a new phase, in which the limits of centralized direction and control are now accepted, and the opportunities for alliances between the public sector and non-governmental entities have never been brighter. The State must still see things in the round, "overseeing the interlocking parts of the national economy and the social system, but governments and leaders of thought, both inside and outside the apparatus of national and local government, must continue to grow in sophistication about the nature of what I have often called the 'enabling environment'."[17]

In retrospect, the Award has been particularly prescient in recognizing examples of the creative use of such an environment, with the Hafsia Quarter in Tunisia, the Ismailiyya Development project in Egypt, Pondok Pesantren Pabelan in Java, the Kampung Improvement Project in Jakarta, the rehabilitation in Asilah, Morocco, and the Grameen Bank Housing Programme in Dhaka, each representing different ways of utilizing it.

Of all the projects premiated for this Fifth Award Cycle, those in the category which was identified in Cairo as "a contemporary architectural expression of quality", which represent "the best efforts at capturing the opportunities of the present and defining our dreams for tomorrow..." are perhaps the most difficult to categorize. It is this indefinable quality, perhaps, which has always precipitated such volatile and constructive debate about where architecture in the Islamic world is, or should be, going as well as the proper relationship it should have to the past. As a clue to the possibilities that have been available, His Highness the Aga Khan, in his opening speech in Cairo, also said in connection with this category, that:

"We strive for appropriate solutions to the problems of today's Muslim societies. Firmly anchored in the present, the best architectural efforts are those that dare to innovate, to start from what we have, and actively invent the future in practical, empowering terms, thereby creating a heritage for the future. Invariably, such efforts do not copy the past, or import solutions developed for other problems and other cultures. What the Muslim world needs today, I suggest, is more of those innovative architects who can navigate between the twin dangers of slavishly copying the architecture of the past and of foolishly ignoring its rich legacy. It needs those who can thoroughly internalise the collective wisdom of

ABOVE: The Asilah Rehabilitation Programme, which won an Award in the Fourth Cycle.

bygone generations, the eternal Message and ethic with which we live, and then reinforce them in the language of tomorrow."[18]

It is interesting to note that, considering the background of the members of the Master Jury, which included three architects who are internationally recognized for their contributions to the freedom of expression that has now come to characterize contemporary design, all the projects premiated in this category seem to be conspicuously supportive of this kind of innovation and collective wisdom. This may be the result of social upheavals in various parts of the world during the last three years, of which the riots in Los Angeles may be seen as a part. The extent to which architecture alone can bring about social change has been an ongoing source of debate since the advent of the industrial revolution, when centralization of specific technologies first brought about the dislocation of entire communities that has now reached its inevitable *dénouement*. As capitalistic imperatives gradually convert the developing world into its industrial equivalent, leaving "the information society" in its wake, people everywhere are trying to cope with the changes that such shifts have caused. In the wake of such transformation, of which the extended global economic correction that is mistakenly being labelled as a recession in both the East and the West is perhaps the most graphic symptom, the high technology, individual architectural effort is more difficult to justify than ever. A heightened awareness of international interdependence, especially in regard to environmental issues such as the equitable use of limited mineral resources, the responsibility for pollution that causes deforestation, desertification and the global warming that results from it, have made architecture using materials that are energy-intensive to produce, let alone expensive to buy or import, increasingly suspect.

All of these factors have seemed to combine in the choices for this cycle, which have rejected the idea of architecture as a finely-crafted object, produced as a one-off to satisfy egotistical motives. In the evolution of this particular category, "quality" as a value judgment is now related entirely to appropriate technology, use of systems, replicability, groupings, local materials, regional craftsmanship, and common sense, and has now been visualized as a way of generating a new architectural language. In each case the winners had to make the most of extremely limited resources, and have dealt with them in an ingenious way.

A New Synthesis and Broader View

Rather than acquiescing to the three categories that have been described here as informing past choices, which were used as a framework for presenting the projects to them, the Jury found that other, more far-reaching similarities between them suggested a different categorization. In their view, the Kairouan Conservation Programme, Palace Parks Programme, Cultural Park for Children in Cairo, East Wahdat Upgrading Programme, and Kampung Kali Cho-de, in a larger sense, all respond to pressing urban problems in ways that should be recognized over and above their more generic characteristics. By grouping them all under the category of "Enhancing Urban Environments", it was felt that this particular aspect, which they all share, would be emphasized to greater effect.

Enhancing Urban Environments

Rather than dwelling on the elements of conservation in the Palace Parks and Kairouan projects already alluded to here, the jury, in choosing to focus on the inspired contribution they have each made to their respective cities, serving as a model for change, has shifted the emphasis of their recognition from the parts to the entirety and to intention rather than means.

When considered in this light, the East Wahdat Upgrading Programme and Kampung Kali Cho-de, which share much in common with the Grameen Bank Housing Programme, given an award in 1989, in terms of relationships to financial institutions and local authorities, are not self-contained instances of entrepreneurial skill, but have broader implications for the urban context around them. In both Yogyakarta and Amman, such settlements were initially considered to be undesirable by public officials, who sought to stop them, but were persuaded to change their opinion by popular support for each project. This support was generated in various ways, in the case of Kampung Kali Cho-de by interest from students of architecture, who analyzed it as a case study, and by the presentation of the project on television as an example of self-help housing. In

26

East Wahdat, the Urban Development Department, who recognized the important relationship between land ownership and the will to improve property brought about this change. This transformation from being outside the system at the beginning, and then eventually achieving acceptance by it, should not be taken lightly as it underlines the institutional changes that are necessary to bring about basic upgrading in overcrowded and unsanitary settlements that have become a familiar part of large cities today.

While the Grameen Bank Housing Programme of the last cycle focused on changes relative to financial institutions, and practices that exclude people below a certain economic level, Kampung Kali Cho-de and East Wahdat point to the need for official recognition of the forces that bring such settlements into existence instead of pretending that they do not exist, or hoping they will miraculously disappear if enough obstructive legislation is passed to prevent them. While attitudes now range from benign disinterest to aggressive disdain, these two particular examples show how such attitudes can change, and this is one key to the success of similar enterprises in the future. A caveat, however, that is highlighted here is that, in spite of similarities, the local context in each instance has imposed specific restrictions of its own, and it would be wrong to imply that obstructions do not remain. The positive public sentiment for Kampung Kali Cho-de has been qualified by a general feeling that the settlement should remain only until such time as permanent housing is available to its residents. The Laboratory of Housing and Human Settlements is presently working with the Government of Surabaya on ways of preventing this kind of settlement in the future. At best, the public and official attitude towards the Kampung can only be characterized as one of tolerance, since it is seen locally as an interim solution to an intractable problem and the best that the people themselves can manage to do until the Government provides a permanent substitute. As the technical reviewer for this project has said: "As a transitory solution it is certainly not wrong. But surely a must is for the residents to adopt self-help as a means of improvement. The result improves the condition of the settlement, increases safety for residents, offers occupation for some and enhances the aesthetic quality of the environment."[19]

ABOVE: A resident of Kampung Kali Cho-de.

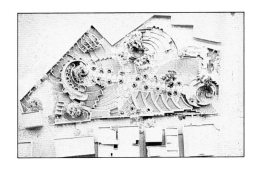

Qualifications of another kind can also be mentioned for East Wahdat, in regard to financing, since unlike the Kampung, the project was approached as a conversion from temporary shelter to permanent housing by both the Urban Development Project and the World Bank, which provided assistance for it. In making this conversion, careful consideration was given to the economic capacity of each family to pay for their specified plot and space needs as well as services. An intricate system of cross-subsidies, reminiscent of those established in other premiated projects in the past, has been implemented with shops and light industrial components located on prime spots around the site, which were offered for sale at market prices. The plot layouts were also planned so that a percentage of the land could be freed for the construction of speculative housing to help finance the remainder of the upgrading. The concepts of recoverable investment, cross-subsidy based on legal tenure, and equity are central to this project, which, like the Grameen Bank Housing Programme in the 1989 cycle, had to be based on personal loans to prospective owners in order to begin. Since the East Wahdat project is prototypical, in the sense that it is a test of the institutional capacity to manage and replicate such communities throughout the country, the viability of this financial concept was doubly important. Unlike the high rate of repayment that has been such a critical factor in the success of the Grameen Bank scheme, the notion of cost recovery has not been so easily assimilated by the residents of East Wahdat, for reasons that are still not clear. On a positive note, however, improved living conditions have been shown to have a direct relationship to rising levels of income in the community from an average of JOD80 (US$272) per month prior to improvement in 1981, to JOD120 (US$408) per month afterwards.

Abrupt change in income level, amounting to a doubling on average, must be taken into consideration when the question of cost-recovery is being considered in this particular instance. Such qualifications show that each situation is unique, and never problem-free. The important lesson provided by Kampung Kali Cho-de and East Wahdat, however, remains clear: that replicable, self-help methods based on existing skills and appropriate local technologies and close co-

ABOVE: The Cultural Park for Children in Cairo is a rare synthesis of architecture and landscape design, and teaches its users about history through innovation rather than imitation.

operation between public agencies and the people themselves can be implemented to house the homeless and dramatically improve the most dire living conditions. The hope that this holds out for people who are homeless, or living in squalor, throughout the world is beyond price.

The Cultural Park for Children in Cairo, Egypt, by Abdelhalim Ibrahim Abdelhalim, which is the fifth project premiated by the Master Jury in their new category of "Enhancement of Urban Environments", will be taken out of its order of citation and discussed last here since it cannot be compared with any other project and nothing like it has ever previously been acknowledged by the Award. Located in Sayyida Zeinab, which was formerly known as the El-Hod El-Marsoud Garden, the park combines architecture and landscape design to a degree that is rare in contemporary experience. Previously the location of the Birket El-Fil in the Mamluk period, this whole area was once covered by an artificial lake surrounded by large houses during the Middle Ages, and was one of the wealthiest parts of Old Cairo. The Ibn Tulun Mosque, with its famous spiral minaret and clearly organized square plan, lies less than 100 metres away to the south. The double-domed tomb of Salar and Sangar Al Gawli, as well as the Sargamish Mosque and Madrasa and the Shaykhun Complex are also in close proximity. The streets and buildings surrounding the site, that is the urban fabric or context, have influenced the architect's design decisions to a remarkable degree, and must be described in further detail to fully appreciate what has been achieved here. As outlined by the technical reviewer for this project, these boundaries include Abu al-Dahab Street, which is a continuation of El-Hod El-Marsoud Street on the north, which is a very historically significant thoroughfare, and Qadry Street to the east, which is more recent and offers an unobstructed view of the Ibn Tulun Mosque because it is relatively straight. Qadry Street offers a short-cut between two important medieval routes: Marrassina to the south of the site links the Citadel Square to Sayyida Zeinab Square; Port Said - formerly El-Khalig El-Masry - links Sayyida Zeinab to al-Azhar and other northern parts of the old city. All of these streets and thoroughfares are now subject to major infrastructure development and traffic modifications. Abu al-Dahab Street consists of several residential blocks with some institutional and industrial buildings, This has largely conserved the architecture of the street which dates from the early 20th century. Several government and public buildings surround the site to the east and south. These include a late 19th century hospital, the municipal headquarters for the district, a training centre for fire and emergency services, and a more recent children's hospital south of the site. Unique examples of institutional and industrial architecture from the early 1900s have been conserved. Yet most of the buildings which surround the site exist in different degrees of dilapidation, although the façades of Abu al-Dahab Street and some of the institutional buildings were upgraded in the context of the Park Project. The initiative to upgrade some areas around the site is viewed as the commencement of a much wider process of upgrading which has been formalized by the local district authorities in co-ordination with the park designer. These proposals have recently been approved for implementation.[20]

The entire area is a perfect example of the deteriorating environment that Professor Arkoun speaks about in this book, with degradation beginning at the time of Mohammed Ali, who drained the Birket el-Fil to make way for additional streets in his wish to pattern the area on Belle Epoque Paris and the grand avenues of Baron Haussmann.

"Intervention" is a popular word in architectural schools today, but Abdelhalim's design really *is* intervention in the most positive sense, meaning to arrest the deterioration that was accelerating here at such a rapid rate and to turn it around. The story of the architect's vision for the scheme, which he has consistently seen as a response to the difficult physical and historical constraints presented to him, is one that is characterized by a mixture of courage and sensitivity, and determination not to allow the formidable bureaucracy he was faced with to defeat him.

The organization of the park revolves around four principles which provided an initial framework for the design and are still legible to a remarkable degree. The first of these, relating to the emblematic aspect of the project, relates to rhythm. In answer to his own question about the similarities between the children who would use the space, and the park itself, the architect saw growth as one possible theme, and the spiral, which demonstrates the laws of growth in nature, as a metaphorical representation of this idea. The second principle is geometry, which is related to the formal, built portions of the park. The architect posed himself questions about the way in which symbols are transformed into order in a way that preserves the original power of the symbol and yet helps to organize the various necessary functional elements that must be dealt with. Once again, the spiral seemed to be a logical choice, given its clear visual dominance in the neighbourhood and its historical significance.

Abdelhalim considered ways in which the three-dimensional spiral of Ibn Tulun could be transformed into a planar matrix across the site, working on two interlocking grids. The first of these began with a line of palm trees that were already growing there, and the other with the streets themselves, in order to join the natural and the man-made. The insistence on the module of the palm trees, which seemed to continue to indicate an order by their measured diagonal march across the open ground, convinced the architect that such a weave was the correct thing to do. The third principle evolved from this mesh and relates to its co-ordinates. To extend the meaning of such a geometry, which has been extracted from both the natural and constructed layers of the existing context, as well as the requirements of the programme, the architect next established a conventional grid that would satisfy all three. As the technical reviewer has noted: "The use of co-ordinates, or Ihdathiyyat, has been shown to be a technique that has frequently been used in the traditional architecture of Egypt, and it relies upon proportion, as well as references such as Ø, which is the equivalent of the golden ratio."[21] The co-ordinate system of the park was extracted from the size of the space between each of the palm trees that still grew along a promenade planned for the site, which as the architect saw it, was the most apparent measure to be used.

The fourth and final principle that has been employed related to the ritualistic or ceremonial aspect of the architecture, which is also central to Abdelhalim's other work, and is based on his research into the connections between built form and culture. His doctoral thesis, as presented at UCLA, Berkeley, in 1978, which was entitled *The Building Ceremony*, was based on this idea and explains how community response to a proposal should determine incremental formal decisions, rather than using the opposite approach, which is normal today, of considering architecture as a *fait accompli* to be presented as a beneficence to people who cannot possibly comprehend its mysteries. In this sense Abdelhalim has much in common with architect Charles Moore, who has been campaigning for community involvement throughout his career, and has remained something of a voice in the wilderness in his belief in the instinctive wisdom of popular opinion for many years. His group sessions, which include clients, regardless of their number, in the design process, are now legendary, and remain the nemesis of many lesser talents who are too insecure to follow him. By proposing such an incremental approach in Sayyida Zeinab, Abdelhalim is perpetuating this idea of popular involvement, which had previously been such a critical ingredient in the growth of the urban environment there in the past.

The architect's own recounting of the difficulties involved in establishing this kind of involvement, of basically changing attitudes and habits which have now been instigated since the time of the industrial revolution, is compelling, and deserves to be presented in its entirety as a perfect example of political rather than aesthetic innovation. As he has described it, there was a protracted lull in activity after his firm was selected by competition until contracts were signed for design development and construction supervision. Funds had been allocated but he subsequently found out that the project had been blocked by "political interest groups in the Parliament". After several confrontations with officials and assurances that the project could continue, there was still no progress, indicating that something was drastically wrong. Then, as he says:

"We soon realized what it was. We had been trying to define the project through public meetings and through the media, but the people in the community, the real supporters of the project, had no contact with either. They were cut off from the press and from the power structure, which in any case was confused about the image of the project and argued against its order and character. We realized that we would have to mobilize the community to get the project moving, not just to defend the project but to build it. We looked for an opportunity to do this.

The opportunity came when the Minister of Culture decided to lay the corner-stone of the project during the National Festival for Children, a celebration held in Egypt in November of each year. Some officials, the architect, and representatives of the local community were scheduled to attend.

Normally, a corner-stone laying is completely detached from the life of the community, but we proposed to the Minister of Culture that, in place of drawings and working models that were usually displayed in a tent on such occasions and which, to most people, were meaningless, a real life-size model of the scheme could be displayed to give the whole community a glimpse of what the project was to look like. The spiral geometry of the fountain, exhibits, museum, and theatre should be constructed in a tent and the platforms and terraces would be marked on the ground by colours. Each element would be mocked-up full scale in its actual place on the site.

In our memorandum to the Minister, we also suggested inviting artists, musicians and folklore dancers to participate. They could propose works suggesting the scheme which could then be performed by schoolchildren from the local community. In this way we sought to restore the age-old function of the building ceremony that had been traditional in Egypt, from the Luxor Temple and mosque of Ibn Tulun almost up to the present day.

The Minister was eventually persuaded by our scheme although mainly because the ceremony was to be attended by the President and his wife and would draw attention to the significant role it was playing in the development of local communities. The image of hundreds of children playing and dancing around the mock-up park and the full-scale model, while tens of thousands of citizens looked on, appealed to the political instincts of the Minister and he approved.

We began by making a set of drawings that would enable the tent builders to produce a tent overnight. On the site, local officials prepared the grounds for the tents, and contracted schools, artists and musicians. Within eighteen hours, a two-and-a-half acre lot had been transformed from a deserted, run-down site into a fabulous scene of tents that beautifully, if not altogether

ABOVE: The spiral motif, taken from the nearby mosque of Ibn Tulun, as well as a modular co-ordinate based on the spacing of pre-existing palm trees, helped to determine the design of the park.

accurately, reproduced the arrangement of the proposed scheme. The children began to arrive to rehearse on the temporary stage that had been set up. For three or four days hundreds of them gathered in groups to practise, while a choreographer and the musicians worked out the performance to follow the configuration of the scheme. When they could not, we changed the scheme's arrangement. This happened several times and each time the scheme was improved. Instead of the original plan disappearing from sight, it continued to evolve in front of me. I came actually to believe what I had claimed to the Minister, that the great buildings of Egypt were always the result of ceremony. Certainly the performance of this festival added something to the plan that rational designing could not have conceived. The action of the community added a sense of wholeness that would otherwise not have been there."[22]

As a result of this emphasis on the age-old significance of the laying of the corner-stone, which dates back to the Pharaonic period, the community was galvanized into action, and their participation in the realization of the park was assured. An important extra benefit of the strategem was that Abu al-Dahab Street was also included into the brief, which has since proved to be critical, since it has extended the psychological territory of improvements carried out in the park across site boundaries and allowed them to reverberate into the residential wall around them, with gratifying results. By treating the edge of the park as a perforated screen, which allows residents to see through it and invites them in, and yet still maintains a necessary degree of security, this interlinking between new and old was reinforced.

The architectural elements of the park recall familiar historical forms without literally copying them, providing commentary on the past without didacticism, and a comfortable continuity. Considering the impressionable nature of the young people using the park, the architecture has been treated as a three-dimensional history lesson, designed as an echo to the many important monuments nearby, encouraging the children to look at both, and to learn by comparison. By avoiding the temptation of derivative transcription, he has allowed the children's imaginations to make the requisite leap between what was and what is, which makes the lesson much more vivid

and enduring. In many cases, because of the absence of rain in Egypt, and the warmth of most days and nights, the "rooms" have purposely been left without a roof to make the structure, and the contrast between architecture and nature, more clear. Teachers use the arches and the orderly geometry of the co-ordinates that are used to teach geometry, particularly al-Khwarazmi's contributions to mathematics; and by learning in the workshops provided, pupils see their lessons as a continuation of their cultural heritage, not as mechanical exercises that are separated from it. This is in keeping with the architect's attitude toward tradition, which he sees as a living thing, as an "envelope" of culture. The methodology of design by accretion puzzled officials connected with the project and did not make the architect's task any easier but the benefits of such an approach have now become obvious and are appreciated by all concerned.[23]

The role of the craftsmen was an integral part of this method, centring around the choice of limestone as the basic material used, to tie the architecture to the Mamluk and Ottoman buildings in the neighbourhood. Once the basic stone structure was established, other craftsmen, such as carpenters, could interpolate from it, and learn in the process.

The Cultural Park for Children has really lived up to its name, exceeding the expectations of the brief and providing an exemplary instance of the integration of architecture and landscape design, as well as proof that the process of decay, which seems endemic to many of the older sections of Cairo, can be reversed.

Generating New Architectural Languages
In its second category of "Generating New Architectural Languages", each of the four projects recognized by the jury share several key characteristics which may be summarized as replicability, use of appropriate technology and local materials, environmental awareness, low-cost construction, an ingenious translation of forms and techniques based on indigenous prototypes, and an effortless blending of system and function. In the case of both the Stone Building System and the Panafrican Institute for Development that translation is from a dialect first reintroduced into contemporary architecture by Hassan Fathy after his visits to Nubian villages

near Aswan in 1943. While the dome and vault system that he discovered there, which may be seen to have been used in Egypt millenia ago, had been publicized by others prior to his reinstitution of it in several private houses, and eventually the village of New Gourna between 1943 and 1945, he was able to coalesce the method in a practical way through an empirical process, finally publishing it in *Construire Avec le Peuple* and *Architecture for the Poor* thirty years later. The critical advantage of the Nubian technique is that it requires no formwork or centring of any kind, relying only on the initial construction of a conventionally laid, vertical kick wall to absorb the compressive thrust of the first vault. The buildings in Burkina Faso, as designed by ADAUA, follow this system, but the forms are more elaborate than the Nubian model, having been influenced by local villages. The quality of the soil has a great deal to do with its suitability for mud-brick construction, and while the clay of the Nile Valley is extremely cohesive, because of continuous sedimentary deposits prior to the construction of the Aswan High Dam, the sandy loam of the Sahel is not, making stabilization necessary. The need for extreme flexibility precluded the use of a compressive kick-wall and so re-usable shuttering was also involved for the rapid construction of the arches. The idea of using stone, instead of the reinforced concrete frame and block infill technique now commonly used throughout the region, conforms to the ancient tradition of stone construction here, with vaults also reflecting the Roman presence in the past. The use of local stone makes sense for several reasons, in terms of environmental performance, due to its high insulation value and thermal absorption and cost, since it reduces expenditure by thirty per cent. There is another interesting historical parallel here, in that Hassan Fathy also tried to develop a prototypical school in Egypt using a vault and dome system, and succeeded in doing so at Faris and Edfu, halfway between Luxor and Aswan. Misrepresentations on the cost of these projects by local contractors fearful that the widespread implementation of this technique would damage their business, hurt Fathy deeply, since it actually cost so little in comparison with conventional methods. His subsequent disillusionment, which he poignantly described in *Architecture for the Poor* was one of

ABOVE: Panafrican Institute for Development, Burkina Faso; Overview of the Demir Holiday Village, as seen from the water; Sketch of the Village by the architect.

the reasons for his leaving Egypt in 1956 in a self-imposed exile that lasted for five years. And so the Stone Building System is not only a tribute to the skill of the three Muhanna brothers but an echoing vindication of Fathy's belief in the principles they represent as well.

Whereas the Panafrican Institute for Development and the Stone Building System represent variations on a structural theme, the two remaining projects in the Jury's category of "New Architectural Languages", while also incorporating local materials, traditional models, and environmental strategies, deal more with groupings, and permutations. The Demir Holiday Village explores various plan types designed to attract buyers to this developing resort, of which they represent the first part. Thirty-five villas, divided into more than twelve different types, range across 2.7 hectares within a fifty-hectare site secured by the architect for future growth. Given the profile of prospective owners for these speculative houses, and their cost, the necessity of treating each plot as a separate entity, to retain an aura of individuality, was of paramount concern. To do so, the architect made the majority of the houses two storey, to conform with local building codes, and negotiated with the authorities to mix in 5% of three-storey and 5% of single-storey houses to give the impression of the randomness of a pre-existing, traditional community, and to convey this singularity. The site plan is a lesson in how to achieve diversity with standardized units, and a dignified architecture with an economy of means and systematic approach. Details such as fenestration, landscaping, patterning of stonework, and paving were also deliberately changed to accentuate variety.

The Entrepreneurship Development Institute of India, in Ahmedabad, is an extension of the lessons about individuality within community conveyed by the Demir villas, and carries them to an institutional level. Because it is in a less benign climate, protective strategies of clustering and enclosure were necessary here, making a large, central courtyard and deeply recessed arcades a logical choice. In this case, the architect, Bimal Patel, has strong opinions about the need to reintroduce a diversity of building types, representative of the numerous forms evident in the history of Islamic architecture, back into contemporary usage. In his studies at Berkeley,

he was particularly keen on deriving organizational principles from past examples, redrawing buildings from *The Archaeological Survey of India* to establish the patterns rather than the exact images of the past. He cites Leon Krier, Klaus Herdeg and Christopher Alexander as his main influences, indicating a rational preference for typologies and "pattern language" over individual expression. While he has also expressed his intention to play down the classical tradition consistently promoted in undergraduate history courses in favour of eastern models, the planning principles used in the layout of the Institute raise interesting questions about inter-relationships between the two, beginning with speculation about vestigial strains still remaining from Alexander the Great, his tenure in India, and promotion of institutional ideals. The theatre, which was originally meant to terminate the composition along its eastern, entrance edge, has not been completed, but lends weight to this line of enquiry, as does the partially axial, partially random character of the groupings. They are, in many ways, reminiscent of the work of Louis Kahn, who has had such a strong impact in this region and whose own assymmetrical symmetry followed models such as Hadrian's Villa in Tivoli. In general the EDII campus attempts to reconcile two historical and institutional directions, with the latter being the need for quiet introspective, private spaces, as well as the clear expression of each part. It succeeds in each to a remarkable extent, with subtlety and strength.

Lessons

Juror Azim Nanji, in discussing the relationships between all of the projects selected in this cycle, has made the observation that, in one way or another, they all relate to education, not in the functional sense, but in their ability to convey a new attitude about architecture. Each speaks to a growing awareness of a change in sensibilities about the role that architecture should play in society, which is much different from the one it has played in the recent past. The aspects of that change, regardless of the category they have been listed in, centre around participation rather than exclusivity, raising serious questions about the position that an architect will have in this process in the future. Precursors of this shift, such as Fathy, have continually, and imploringly, warned of the dangers of preciousness and egoism, encouraging architects to think in terms of partnership with their clients, rather than of complete aesthetic control, in any project. As he has emphasized, this was normally the case, prior to the industrial revolution, when the symbiotic links between master builder and those for whom the building was intended, were broken. The re-establishment of this connection, as it is symbolized in each of the projects presented here, is striking and significant, whether it be the pragmatically direct co-operation required in the upgrading of a squatter settlement, or the restoration of historic fabric.

These portents do not predict that architects are now an extinct species, or even an endangered one, but that they must evolve to survive. Of all the challenges presented by this fifth cycle, this is perhaps the most striking.

Notes

1. Mohammed Arkoun, "Islamic Cultures, Developing Societies, Modern Thought" from *Expressions of Islam in Buildings*, Proceedings of an International Seminar sponsored by the Aga Khan Award for Architecture and the Indonesian Institute of Architects, Jakarta, Indonesia, October, 1990, The Aga Khan Trust for Culture, 1990, p.49

2. Ibid., p.49

3. Speech by His Highness the Aga Khan at the Fourth Ceremony of the Aga Khan Award for Architecture, Cairo, 15 October, 1989

4. Sherban Cantacuzino, "Conservation in the Social Context", Papers in Progress, Vol. 1, *Architectural and Urban Conservation in the Islamic World*, The Aga Khan Trust or Culture, 1990, p.55

5. Tanvir Hasan, Technical Review Report submitted to the Aga Khan Award for Architecture on the National Palaces Programme, Geneva, 1992

6. Ibid.

7. Mohammed Arkoun, "The Meaning of Cultural Conservation in Muslim Societies", Papers in Progress, op. cit., pp.25, 26

8. William C. Clark, "Managing Planet Earth", *Scientific American*, September 1989, Vol. 261, No. 3, p.20

9. Ibid., p.20

10. Chris Abel, "Regional Transformations", *Architectural Review*, November 1986, Vol. 180, No. 1077

11. Chris Abel, Paper to be presented to the Third International Conference of the Association for the Study of Traditional Environments: *Development versus Tradition*, Paris, 8-11 October 1992

12. Ibid.

13. Ibid.

14. M.F. Strong, *Ecodevelopment*, United Nations Environment Programme, UNEP/6C/80, January 1976

15. Chris Abel, op. cit.

16. Ibid.

17. Speech by His Highness the Aga Khan in Cairo, op. cit.

18. Ibid.

19. Johan Silas. *Technical Review Report*, Aga Khan Award for Architecture, Geneva, 1992

20. Jamel Akbar, *Technical Review Report*, Aga Khan Award for Architecture, Geneva, 1992

21. Ibid.

22. Abdelhalim I. Abdelhalim, as quoted in the *Technical Review Report*, Aga Khan Award for Architecture, Geneva, 1992

23. See: Jamel Akbar, "Accretion of Decisions: A Design Strategy", *Theories and Principles of Design in the Architecture of Islamic Societies*, Proceedings of a Symposium held at Harvard University and M.I.T., edited by B. Sevcenko, Cambridge, Mass., 1988, pp. 107-114.

Suha Özkan
A PLURALIST ALTERNATIVE

As have so many other disciplines, the architectural profession has undergone dramatic changes over the past twenty years. Inevitable and unalterable transformations have required all those involved with architecture to re-define the profession, its scope as well as its discourse, and to accommodate any number of new and unexpected situations, some of them of an urgent nature. The validity and effectiveness of the profession were put under harsh scrutiny, as discourse seemed eventually to reveal increasing uncertainty and ever-penetrating probity: "What", was always asked, "is architecture, and what is the proper role of an architect?" In response, new concepts and new terms emerged, as architects assumed the roles of "agents of change", "social advocates", "enablers", and "decision-makers" in addition to their more poetic place in the field of fine arts, as designers, artists, sculptors of form. Architecture itself, as Sir Nicholas Pevsner postulated, lay between a bicycle shed and a cathedral, and the definition of architecture began to simultaneously accommodate a wide range of alternatives: *Architecture without Architects* (B. Rudofsky), *Unselfconscious Design* (C. Alexander), *Shelter and Society* (P. Oliver), as well as *Freedom to Build* and *Housing by People* (J. Turner).

This new sense of questioning was not, however, shared by all, and a small elite continued to fashion prestigious - and often exquisite - commissions which were lavishly published in glossy journals; alas, these noble artefacts, like the expensive journals, had little impact on or relevance to the vast majority. The rampant growth of the built environment had surpassed professional architects; much lay in the hands of mercantile developers, but the largest part fell to the individuals, communities, and societies. Those lacking most in means and abilities, were also most in need, and thus undertook the provisioning of their own environments in whatever fashion possible, whether legal or not, reflecting their own needs, aspirations, and tastes. This was nowhere more evident, as it is today and promises to be tomorrow, than in the Third World.

During the recent past, it is the urban environ-ments that have suffered most tragically, although the rural areas have not escaped ravage and disintegration. The irreversible process of change has rapidly altered the natural as well as the built environment, and predictions for the future warn that this disfigurement will continue at an alarming rate.

Meanwhile, the architectural elite continue their weighty discourse and seek to re-instil meaning and significance into an architecture which they feel has been robbed by the so-called "Modern Movement". The debate is highly charged, heavily rhetorical, and strongly laced with finely-tuned semantics. And, in the meantime, the cries of hundreds of millions remain unheard, and can have but little hope in an architectural profession seemingly enchanted only with itself. It never deigns to see, much less tackle, the plight of decaying cities, inadequate services, and the homeless many.

Still, the lonely voices of the concerned few pointed to the resources of traditional processes and patterns which had, in the past, resulted in suitable, if not always perfect, built environments, usually endowed with authentic cultural richness, and often attaining harmony and beauty. The role of individuals and societies in determining their own environment, loudly voiced by Turner, helped foster the concept of "appropriate technology" which depended upon people themselves and the recognition that their own participation was the only available resource on which they could truly rely. That resource continues to be a formidable one.

Once again, the architectural elite turned a deaf ear, and relegated such concepts to the realm of anthropology, leaving others to worry about urban and rural shelters, or cultural heritage.

Nevertheless, a few flames of hope illuminated the wilderness. Hassan Fathy had begun the valiant call for an "architecture for the poor". Charles Correa sought an architecture sensitive to the climate with his slogan "form follows climate". He implicitly nurtured the legacy of Jane Drew and Maxwell Fry who had tried to adapt the grand strategies of Le Corbusier to the realities of India and to implement their own ideas in Africa. In London, Otto Koenigsberger remained dedicated to the training of "alternative" architects capable of encouraging environmentally sensitive architecture and of coping with the emerging realities of the urban dilemma. André Ravereau and Roland Simounet began serious efforts in the Maghreb, and Geoffrey Bawa undertook a similar self-committed mission in the lush tropics of Ceylon. In Turkey, Sedad Eldem sought a modern identity for the traditional Turkish house, and in Bangladesh, Muzharul Islam concentrated on developing an architectural expression reliant upon limited resources and affordable technology. Rifat Chadirji in Baghdad strove to develop a culturally rich architectural idiom of his own. And in concert, many of those concerned came together under such leaders as Doxiadis and the Ekistics Center in order to attempt a re-formulation of urban planning.

For the most part, the western media and profession remained sceptical at best, and ignorant of these pioneers and the emerging consciousness that had produced them. It was not until the 1970s that public awareness in the West began to awaken to the need for environmental protection and to focus on the imperatives of human rights. Around this time, the notion of a "master plan", as a sort of heaven-sent panacea, began to give way as people themselves became active advocates for and participants in the shaping of their own environments.

It was in the midst of this confused state of affairs that the Aga Khan took the initiative to actively encourage the built environment and architecture of Muslims. With a small group of architects, thinkers, and scholars, he elaborated an award committed to exploring architecture in Muslim societies and to identifying worthy examples there that merit encouragement and demonstrate to others possible solutions and approaches which might be applied elsewhere. Thorough and meticulous procedures were put into place for the documentation and evaluation of building projects, and a series of seminar meetings was organized on a regular basis in order to enhance and nurture the learning process. The seminar topics were widely varied, from housing to symbolism, from architectural education to the architecture of public places, and focused on urban centres as well as the rural habitat. At each meeting, international participants joined local architects, planners, and others to share ideas and establish dialogue. Site visits were organized as an important component of every meeting, and provided first-hand testimony of the actual condi-

tions at every seminar locale. The chosen venues where the seminars were organized demonstrated the wide variety of cultures, climates, and geographies of the Muslim world: from Central Java to Andalusia, from North Africa to China, from Cairo to Malta, to Sana'a, to Dakar, to Istanbul. And the published proceedings of every seminar were widely distributed to further increase the scope of participation and interest and to provide the widest possible access to the thoughts and ideas.

Four award cycles have been completed since 1978. Twelve international and three regional seminars have been held. Over two million dollars have been awarded by the consecutive Master Juries to forty-eight building projects, and two special awards have honoured the life-long work of Hassan Fathy and Rifat Chadirji. A wealth of material has resulted from the study of candidate buildings and the documentation centre established in Geneva is the most comprehensive and important facility of its kind in the world.

When seen together, the seemingly disparate building projects that have received awards, and the topics of all of the seminars, reveal a number of key issues and focal points that remain at the heart of the Aga Khan Award for Architecture: architectural heritage, cultural identity, environmental and climatic awareness, continuity with the past, reality of the present and contemplation of the future, appropriate technology, and social and environmental harmony.

The very first cycle soundly tested the established programme and procedures, and confirmed the Award's reputation not only as the world's most prestigious, but also as its most determined and serious architectural award. From 1978 to 1980, five international seminars were held in Paris, Istanbul, Jakarta, Fez, and Amman, bringing together the widest possible range of those involved in the shaping of the built environment. As never before, a platform for serious enquiry was opened without the restraints - and without the fear - of governments, politics, and officialdom, yielding a critical debate on issues of the utmost concern. The contributors to the emerging dialogue were a curious mix of architects, technicians, scholars, and everyday people concerned with their environment. They represented a wide spectrum, from little-known and emerging talents to the most celebrated international architects, from East to West and North to South, from modest masons to heads of state, from behavioural scientists to financial planners, and included women as well as men, the young as well as the old, and any number of languages, cultures and races. In short, it gathered together the rich range of contrasts and variety that constitute contemporary Islamic societies.

Interest continued to be generated, and the media came to be curious about this peculiar new enterprise. By the time the first awards were announced in Lahore in 1980, considerable enthusiasm had been aroused in anticipation of what many expected would be modern-day equivalents of the Taj Mahal or the Alhambra. And, indeed, the awards came as a surprise. There were, to begin with, fifteen of them, and, alongside impressive examples of contemporary design trends, figured slum quarters, simple housing, a modest school, stretching from Senegal to Indonesia. The jury citations emphasized the notion of "search", and proudly presented this disparate group of fifteen buildings as notable achievements that contributed to the quest for excellence in the built environment. The conception of the Award as an ongoing process, embracing a panoply of concerns and divergent directions, has become a central tenet of the organization and, combined with the "space of freedom" created by the seminar forums, the notions of quest and process came to identify the Award above and beyond the recognition of individual buildings and the attribution of the half-million dollar prize fund.

The emphasis placed by the first jury on encouraging community efforts had two important effects: firstly, it served as a source of inspiration, pride, and encouragement for some of the world's poorest communities, by acknowledging their efforts to create their own living environments. Secondly, it brought such efforts to the attention of the architectural profession and the world at large and, most importantly, accorded them a status equal to that of any other example of good architecture. These same motivations would be reinforced by all of the subsequent juries who continued to appreciate and to honour community efforts and commitments to life, family, and well-being.

Not only was the upgrading and improvement of poor communities a focus, but the provision of new and appropriate housing has been a constant concern of all Award cycles. On a variety of scales related to meeting the needs of all levels of society, the various housing projects demonstrate a great variety of design approaches in both urban and rural contexts, and the levels of technology employed reflect traditional as well as contemporary standards, usually addressing craftsmanship as well as structural systems, and always emphasizing the basic need for shelter, for the poor, for the rich, and for all those in between.

Throughout, appropriate technology has been a feature of the premiated buildings and, once again, the vast array of applications testifies to the diversity of societies comprising the Islamic world. Daring and innovative, some of the awards reveal the most sophisticated use of modern technology anywhere in the world. In Jeddah or in Paris, these marvels of invention have demonstrated the Award's concern for progress and the exploration of often-pioneering directions for future development. In turn, too, the time-honoured traditions and techniques that have not changed for centuries reveal the application of appropriate technology combined with an inherent respect for the past. The mud mosques in West Africa, for example, call on the skills and talents of artisans whose knowledge has been transmitted from generation to generation, to remain as vital today as many centuries ago. Innovation and authenticity have combined in developing an intermediate technology represented by many other winning projects. Drawing on the skills, resources, and materials at hand, these talented efforts often exploit traditional techniques, improving on them slowly and economically, often helping to train new craftsmen in the process, and making new techniques and applications available to others to replicate and modify as specific conditions require and resources permit.

Re-interpretation of past approaches to design, construction, and technology, as well as traditional functions and programmes to contemporary contexts, embody many other winning projects. These, too, have been vehicles to further enhance traditional skills or to express traditional forms in new styles. Contextualism, at both urban and rural scales, has been an important way of establishing continuity with the past while contributing to the rapid advances of twentieth-century life. Inspiration has been drawn from the full breadth of the architectural heritage of Islam, as well as from the specific styles and forms that developed uniquely in its diverse historic societies.

Care and concern for the splendid legacy of past eras are evidenced in every cycle of the Awards, and the restoration and conservation of monuments and historic areas has drawn wide attention. The encouragement of traditional skills and crafts, often in danger of disappearing, is an important component of these projects. The economic revitalisation of historic areas has been of special note, as has the use of some buildings for new functions. These awards have helped show that, with sensitivity and care, historic monuments and areas can once again become vital and dynamic components of contemporary society, blending the past with the present.

And yet, the Award has not been able to address several areas of great importance. Industrial facilities, transportation networks, and major infrastructural efforts are conspicuously absent amongst the winning projects, even though they are increasingly evident in environments throughout the world. Weakly represented, too, are health facilities, and landscaping efforts and open public spaces, although a notable project in Saudi Arabia demonstrated the potential for using natural elements with sensitivity and success in the landscaping of a desert setting for an important new development.

Since its inception, the Award has sought to address the manifold and complex factors contributing to today's architecture. The geographic span of winning projects, the multiplicity of building types, and the range of societal issues addressed have yielded a pluralism much wider and much richer than has previously been encompassed in the domain of architecture. The danger of permitting this sense of pluralism to deteriorate into complaisance has been avoided by the creative and well-considered structuring which reinforces the relevance and validity of each of its component parts. The sense of critical debate and the efforts of committed and concerned individuals working earnestly together to achieve a common goal have helped ensure a sense of purpose and meaning. With integrity and, at times, audacity, the Award has attempted

to discover and to understand contemporary architecture in Islamic societies and has hopefully contributed to the larger effort of encouraging its enhancement and, thereby, the lives of many.

Mohammed Arkoun
ARCHITECTURAL ALTERNATIVES IN DETERIORATING SOCIETIES

His Highness the Aga Khan created the Award for Architecture in order that Muslim societies can speak about themselves, and freely express their concerns, their problems, their aspirations, and their dreams, as well as their failures, their regressive processes, their wrong solutions, their refusals, their violence. The Award listens carefully to these varied and changing expressions without imposing value judgments, without preferring any expression over the other, and without adopting any philosophical or political vision which excludes the new trends and new alternatives that are emerging in so many societies.

We are now celebrating the fifth Award cycle. As has been clearly established during the previous cycles, we once again see the Award's continuing intellectual endeavour, the same open attitude and attentiveness, the same eager but patient will to make explicit, in a relevant, modern language that is far from any polemical or arrogant position, the messages that are implicit in the present architectural alternatives.

The Master Jury of this fifth cycle has been guided in their process of evaluation by a particularly clear and coherent diagnosis: for the past twenty or thirty years, all Muslim societies have been engaged in deteriorating, disintegrating, and regressive mechanisms which simultaneously affect all levels of politics, the economy, culture, education, and society. More and more architects - as well as engineers, teachers, writers, artists, and journalists - are aware of this dramatic trend and are struggling to find new answers and new strategies to stop it, if possible, or at least to limit the negative effects of all the disintegrating forces which are operating at all levels of society.

During the 1960s, many architects ignored or disdained the needs and expectations of the uprooted segments of rural populations which had moved to the urban centres. They built ugly, collective housing characterized by low rent, low life and low culture. This is evident everywhere in the suburbs of many cities in what was previously called the "free" world, in the societies of Eastern Europe, and, of course, in Third World societies. In the Third World, demographic pressure, increasing impoverishment, the corruption of so-called "political elites", the total lack of democracy, and oppressive systems of exploitation combining international systems of exchange with national and local disorder, have generated the physical deterioration of buildings, streets, and urban tissues and facilities. By this continuous process of contamination, the whole environment, both in the larger metropolises and in rural areas, has been affected.

We must clearly identify the determinant factors which have imposed this deterioration throughout the so-called "Muslim societies". One of the great merits of all the Award Master Juries during the five Award cycles is that they have never linked these deteriorating factors with Islam or with what is currently described as fundamentalist, integrist, or radical Islam. Rather, they have suggested that the extremist expressions of Islam are themselves an *effect* and not a *cause*, as is often suggested by political scientists. This means that there is a process of *mental* deterioration accompanying the physical deterioration in the societies we are considering.

The determinant factors which any further critical analysis should consider are:

- The international monetary system.

- The economic strategies imposed by the leadership of the rich, industrialized countries.

- The failure of the "national" elites who have monopolized decision-making processes without giving the people the slightest chance to participate, and without even listening to their claims or their various expressions of suffering or distress[1].

- The mass educational system which imposed political and religious slogans on generations of young people (especially in countries like Egypt, Iraq, Syria, Algeria, and Morocco where 75% of the population was born after 1960).

- Substitution, on a very large sociological scale, of integrated and integrating *pular* and *urban* cultures as they existed everywhere in Muslim societies before 1950-1960 by a *populist* distintegrated culture. It is unfortunate that even scholars are often reluctant to foster positive communication between different linguistic spheres. The French elaboration of the concept "populist/populism" is richer and more operative, for our purposes here, than the same words in English.

- The increasing impoverishment of society as a whole, making it impossible for even students and professors or researchers to have access to scientific books, modern literature and works of art; the great majority of people are prisoners of the fantasy of the discourses, representations, and images broadcast by the media. Books are too expensive or simply unavailable, while populist literature such as pamphlets, so-called religious stories, and religious texts, and the imagery widely expressed in songs, magazines, and radio are, on the contrary, more and more widespread in even the remotest villages.

- Structural violence is, more and more often, replacing the traditional, coherent and efficient codes of culture, ethics, and religion. These value systems - codes of honour and social solidarity - have been maintained for centuries in Muslim societies in rural areas. One example is the highly elaborate cultural codes, called *adab*, observed by the educated classes in urban areas. The disintegration of these codes has taken place over the past thirty years, but more radically over the past twenty years.

In light of this new situation, what are the alternatives proposed by local, committed, concerned architects?

The Master Jury of the current Award cycle proposed the following statements as leit-motifs for the nine winning projects:

- All of the architects had to struggle against bureaucracy, characterized by administrative officers who were unaware of the problems involved, who adhered to rules, norms, and constraints that were irrelevant to the cases at hand, the needs expressed, and the solutions proposed. At the same time, the architects all had to gain the support, at varying levels, of the local authorities.

- The architects all reverted to the use of local skills and locally-available materials instead of imported cement and steel, which are more currently used and provided by industrial firms. Also, they had to train the local users and residents to participate in the various building operations in order for them to share in the collective respect for their newly created environment.

- The architects all strive to improve the living conditions of low-income communities, not with standard units designed in big offices with a complete disregard for the habits, culture, and needs of the new users, but with the ambition "to develop a national capacity to manage such projects and replicate them, in the face of continuing urban growth", "to build a bridge between a marginal refugee population and official institutions", and "to encourage a process of self-help amongst a community used to meeting its own needs for shelter", as has been stated in the jury citation for the East Wahdat Upgrading Programme.

- They aim at "humanitarian and socio-economic development... in a neighbourhood of honest - albeit poor - people, proud of their achievements - the humanization of what were *de-humanized segments* of society", as cited for the Kampung Kali Cho-de.

- Instead of anonymous, standard, administrative buildings, they have attempted to give a sense of dignity, pride and belonging, to children, students and parents by introducing new images and forms, by restoring collective memory, lost skills, and shared aesthetics as can be seen in the Stone Building System, and by helping transform a young, jobless population into business owners (Entrepreneurship Development Institute of India). This Institute deserves special mention because it points to a major ideological mistake which was repeated in so many developing countries during the 1960s and 1970s. This is the famous "socialist, collective model" as imposed in the former Soviet Union and its satellites, and transferred to transitional societies by wilful regimes such as those in Algeria, Tanzania, or the Guinea of Sekou Touré. After gaining political sovereignty, the previously colonized countries needed just what the Institute of Ahmedabad has provided since 1987: to endow each citizen with a sense of responsibility through secured ownership, and a sense of freedom through the actual practice of entrepreneurship which is protected, encouraged, and honoured by the state, and stimulated and promoted by individual initiatives. This was, historically, the social, economic, and educational process by which the European bourgeoisie enhanced democratic regimes. Here, we recognize and understand the deep ideological forces which have led the developing societies into their present state of deterioration, subjected as they were to disabling policies, while European societies have continued, since the 18th century, to foster enabling economic, social and cultural policies of their own.

- The Palace Parks Programme and the Kairouan Conservation Programme point to aspects of the architectural struggle in deteriorating societies. Obviously, the Master Jury wanted to corroborate the coherence of *a single* message - which is not *their* message, but one conveyed by the convergent efforts of architects in several parts of the world. It is a message which is not only particular to Muslim societies in their present phase, but one that also concerns the most developed and sophisticated societies.

How do contemporary societies relate to their past? Do they use the past ideologically, apologetically, and fancifully or according to a critical, responsible, and coherent knowledge of history? If we consider, for example, the significance which European societies since the 19th century have placed on "popular arts and traditions" in their museums (*Musées des Arts et Traditions Populaires* as they are called in France), we discover an arbitrary ideological definition of "popular culture" imposed by the powerful, rich, and educated bourgeoisie. This is being revised now. When we consider "Muslim" societies, we are struck, at first, by the profound and enduring discontinuities since the emergence of an "Islamic" state. It is not the place, here, to elaborate on this very important historical and sociological fact, which has not yet been fully considered in conservation and restoration efforts?

As stated by the Master Jury, the main problem is to find a way "to return a body of monuments (or a whole city, such as Kairouan, Fez, Cairo or Lahore) to the public in terms of history and aesthetics and to produce a system that perpetuates its maintenance". This approach is not sufficient, because it does not include in its thinking process the historical and psycho-sociological concept of the *irreversible*, the *rupture* or *discontinuities*, the *semiotic shifts*, and the *structuring* and *de-structuring* processes at work in all societies and all cultures as changing systems of signs, symbols and signals.

The Palace Parks Programme and the Kairouan Conservation Programme illustrate these views. Apart from purely architectural and urban considerations, the success of conservation and restoration efforts depends on concomitant efforts to restore the historical and cultural conscience of the users in each environment. Teachers, re-searchers, artists, writers, and historians all have a responsibility to explain to their societies the attitudes of mind, the procedures, and the concepts required to have an effective, productive relationship between the past, the present, and the future. This has not been done even in old, well-educated and established European societies.

The historical dimensions of Kairouan, like many old cities in the Muslim world, are far from being fully known. Which period, and which aspects of history and the urban fabric, should be restored? Which of them have actually been restored? How does one insert and link these aspects to the ruptured contemporary structure, especially when the younger generation's historical priorities are so very different from the values re-asserted in some of the restored houses, monuments, or quarters?

There is a necessary follow-up to each attempt at conservation or restoration. It is necessary to know how people receive these initiatives, how they actually use them, how they are inspired by them, whether they remain marginalized, unconcerned, or even opposed to them. Is tourism only for profit or can it be used for a serious cultural exchange between peoples belonging to different loyalties and pasts?

Modesty, low profile, poverty, misery, humiliation, discontinuities, lack of participa-tion, inaccessibility, frustrations, slums, deterioration, disintegration, marginalization, bureaucracy, corruption, oppression ... this is the vocabulary more currently used to describe contemporary "Muslim" societies and it can be enlarged to include Third World societies.

Restoration, conservation, humanization, continuation, re-activation, insertion of tradition in modernity, salvation, help, solidarity, dignity, pride, legitimacy, recovery, renaissance, awakening - is the positive lexicon that is opposed to this negative one.

Architects are not alone in using this parallel or dialectic terminology. Intellectuals, writers, economists, journalists, and politicians cannot avoid it and repeat it so con-stantly that one has to ask if it is a rhetorical exercise or if it reflects concrete changes, positive evolutions, and relevant solutions to pressing problems.

Of all these professions, successful architects have the privilege of achieving con-crete results: they shape the environment, create spaces, forms, places where people can achieve evolutionary behaviour, emancipating thoughts, a creative existence.

Unfortunately, all architects are not successful in this way; clients have a role to play in imposing more effective conditions that go beyond the local, conjunctural, ephemeral solutions suggested by the paralleled opposition between the two sets of such negative/positive vocabulary. This question of clients has not been either correctly or seriously addressed in previous cycles of the Award. With it, we come back to society as a whole in all its various segments and categories; and with society, we raise again the issues of culture and politics in contemporary "Muslim" societies.

If we consider critically each concept or notion conveyed by each of the words listed above, we are obliged to recognize that Islamic thought in its various linguistic spheres (Arabic, Turkish, Persian, Urdu) has not yet crossed ethical, religious or political boundaries to reach an intellectual, scientific field. Tradition and modernity are still used in a dichotomous, dualist opposition, while both concepts are subjected to a new, radical anthropological re-evaluation. This is why I often insist on the unthinkable and the as yet unthought in contemporary Islamic thought. Societies suffer, of course, from this intellectual vacuum left by the rhetorical repetitions of all those who refer endlessly to tradition without having any concrete historical or anthropological knowledge of it.

Here I should like to add another concept to be considered by architects as well as intellectuals, artists and politicians. What I mean is traditionalisation as opposed to living tradition. Tradition in deteriorating societies cannot be restored or reactivated in all its integrating functions in societies not yet fragmented by modern economic systems of production and exchange. It can only be isolated with selected aspects set apart from the deteriorated environment or the modernized segments of society. Good examples are the mosques built by El Wakil in isolated landscapes, or modern architecture without its semiological environment. This practice is called traditionalisation; the so-called Muslim states favour this manipulation of tradition and extend it to law, economics (the so-called Islamic banks), education and politics; that is why my friend Hisham Sharabi is right to develop his concept of neopatriarchy, a theory of distorted change in Arab society.[3] Neopatriarchy is generated by the political will to disguise fragments of modernity imposed by the modern economy and modern technology. Pieces or elements of tradition are juxtaposed or inserted in an urban space or social environment, and are ravaged by deteriorating, distorting, disintegrating forces operating in mentalities, collective behaviour, discourse, physical landscapes, villages, houses, and religious beliefs. I do not know to what extent the members of the Master Jury of this fifth cycle have raised and used this holistic view of the contemporary or so-called "current" Muslim societies.

The initial idea of the Aga Khan Award remains fascinating because it leads all social agents working in Muslim societies, but especially architects, to take into consideration the difficult issue of integrating disintegrating activities in deteriorating societies. It is not sufficient to identify excellence in a building, or relevance in a house, a school, or a kampung. It is more important to explain, in a critical analysis of each project, its ultimate function in society as a holistic system of forces. These operate either to accelerate the disintegration process, or to limit it, or eventually to stop it and initiate a new integrating process. It is clear that neopatriarchy or traditionalisation is overwhelmingly dominating, operating to different degrees and at different speeds in all so-called Muslim societies. It affects official ideologies, state decision-making, private enterprises, various social groups and even intellectuals. It is a powerful, holistic trend given added efficiency by the current economic and political crisis in the seven major First World powers.

However, this historical trend that affects many societies is both intellectually and culturally irrelevant in comparison with the Classical Islamic tradition, or modernity in its emancipating, innovative and positive discoveries. Deteriorating societies ignore both sides: what Classical Islam is historically as an integrating culture and civilization; and what modernity is anthropologically as a holistic view of human history and, consequently, a controlled, critical strategy for emancipating the human condition.

These are the yet unthought, and even unthinkable issues in contemporary deteriorating societies. But have they been better thought out or more correctly addressed in the so-called developed societies, especially in Europe, where modernity in its anthropological dimension emerged for the first time from 1650-1680 onwards, and imposed its positive and negative models? My contention is that the five different Master Juries for the five cycles have not analyzed this level of reflection with respect to the position of deteriorating societies that confront the positive and negative forces of what we call modernity. They have opted for either the recognition of excellence, which is the dominant view among leading architects, or, especially in the present cycle, for what I would call architecture for giving back, for restoring dignity to the brutalized, distressed, populist societies. But they have not yet revealed the hidden mechanism, operating at different levels within various social, political and economic agents. This, in the name of modernity, leads precisely to their deteriorated dignity which is supposed to be protected and restored through architectural efforts such as those premiated here.

We keep repeating that the Aga Khan Award is the unique forum where architects and urbanists can confront each other with their views, theories and experiences. In the case of historians, sociologists, anthropologists, political scientists, philosophers and even theologians, the style of thinking required by deteriorating societies could not be developed productively, concretely, or efficiently. Architects - apart from some admirable ones - have neither the time, nor perhaps the intellectual motivation to engage in the many fields of knowledge affecting the societies where they are supposed to bring solutions to complex problems. Since its first step towards the provision of a space for free research and exchange leading to knowledge and critical analysis, the raising of issues and directions of new thinking so that developing/deteriorating societies are not left to the destructive impact of blind, arbitrary mechanisms, the Award has attempted to do this by, for example, putting together the concepts of developing and deteriorating for the first time since the late sixties. Then, when we spoke of underdeveloped, backward or developing societies, we could not consider development in the traditional, archaic sense as we were still Muslim societies in the midst of the deteriorating process. Now, in overpopulated cities and villages, in oppressive, plethoric bureaucracies, in rigid neopatriarchical institutions, in devastating collective misery, in the increasing crisis facing the educational system, we see the obvious manifestations of deterioration more clearly. We are obliged to rethink the whole issue of development as a dialectic process, not between underdevelopment linked to traditional systems and development bringing modernity, but rather as a struggle between a holistic development encompassing all segments, all levels of human existence, and fragmented sectoral development causing a generalized deterioration of society. No one would deny that architects and urbanists play a major role in this struggle between two opposing concepts which each lead to a different historical evolution. And I do not see any way of escaping the debate on modernity as it operates in the "advanced" rich societies or the model of development/deterioration it imposes on disenabled, manipulated, exploited societies.

These are proposals or appeals to enrich our debates, exchanges and efforts in the free spaces provided by the Aga Khan Award and to permit us to take advantage of the specific opportunities offered by the seminars, the chairs for teaching, the publications, the vast and unique documentation collected over the past fifteen years in the Geneva office. Architecture is a solid, indisputable ground for developing a new approach, for creative thinking about the present stage of historical evolution in all Muslim societies. Architecture can be diverted from its positive contributions to this evolution by overwhelming ideological forces; but it can also resist these forces and offer durable, emancipating answers to the irrepressible hopes and legitimate expectations of future generations. I will even venture to say that architecture today, in Muslim societies, can be an efficient alternative to the models claimed by fundamentalist movements but this cannot happen if architecture continues to be controlled by the aristocratic spirit of the Beaux-Arts.

Notes

1. Already at the end of the sixties, an intelligent and courageous Egyptian sociologist, described a very significant, symbolic expression of suffering in his books *Zahirad al-Murasala il darih al sfa'i* and *Hutaf al-Samitin*. The first is a collection of letters sent by Egyptian peasants to the tomb of Shaf'i', a famous jurist; in these letters, each one introduces a case which he could not expose to the court or the administration; the second is a collection of wishes written by taxi-drivers in their cars.
2. Mohammed Arkoun, *Ouverture sur l'Islam*, 2ème édition, Paris, 1992
3. Hisham Sharabi, *Neopatriarchy: A Theory of Distorted Change in Arab Society*, Oxford University Press, 1987

Fayoum (Gouache by Hassan Fathy).

James Steele
A TRIBUTE TO HASSAN FATHY

Hassan Fathy died in his sleep on 30 November, 1989, and the final chapter in his long and remarkable life has now been closed. During his professional career, which began with his graduation from the University of Cairo in 1926, he was caught up in the end of an era, as well as the emergence of Egypt as a modern state. He lived through occupation, world war, revolution, and the beginnings of a search for a national identity, within a new international order. Because of his deep love for his country, as well as his rare ability to place momentous changes objectively within a wider historical pattern, he did his utmost to assist in that search. Throughout his life, he struggled to ensure that this new identity which continues to evolve, would reflect the best elements of both the past and the present, in order to truly express the cultural richness and complexity that is the essence of Egypt rather than the foreign materialistic values that are completely alien to it. His efforts were tragically misunderstood by the majority of his countrymen, as well as by others throughout the developing world, because to those without his wider perspective, he seemed to stand in direct opposition to the kind of progress deemed to be so vitally important in the three decades following World War II. He was considered by the people who were empowered to implement his ideas to be a hopelessly sentimental romantic. Even worse, he was perceived as a dangerous iconoclast by building contractors who saw his calls for self-help housing and mud-brick architecture as a direct threat to their livelihood. The active resistance to his projects that he frequently alluded to, as well as the numerous accounts of the destroyed careers of those who did believe in him, were both very real.

Because of his unshakeable belief in the validity of tradition, he also stood virtually alone against the Modern Movement that began to gather strength on the Continent just as he started to practise architecture, and he remained a lone, prophetic voice in the wilderness, speaking against it as it began to spread. Any suggestion that Hassan Fathy shared the views of this movement is an affront to his principles and everything he stood for; yet it would be equally inaccurate to assume that his opposition to it implied any doubts on his part about the important role that science and technology must play in architecture. His most vehement criticism of Modernism, in all of its permutations, was its total disregard for human needs and social values, and he held it directly accountable for the wholesale destruction of long-established cultural patterns that such disregard has now encouraged. He also focused on what he considered to be another major failure of Modernism by constantly pointing out its inability to fulfil a self-declared mandate to derive an architecture that would provide clear answers to both physical and environmental laws. Examples of this failure are now legion. In dramatic contrast to the inability of modern architecture to both understand and reflect these unbendable laws, Fathy's own work stands as an eloquent tribute to the seemingly endless degrees of expression offered to those who both accept and work within them, in a knowledgeable, respectful and sensitive way. The form of this architecture, rather than being simply a highly stylized outcome of functional and structural requirements, as it is in Modernist doctrine, becomes primarily answerable to natural forces, as the best vernacular construction has always been. As Fathy himself once said in a lecture at Dar al Islam:

"If the architect does not respect the God-made environment, he commits a sin against God. The God-made environment is the landscape; the atmosphere, the flora, the fauna, and the human beings who live in this environment. In this God-made environment there is nothing that is inharmonious. If we become one with nature, beauty is defined as it is. Beauty, then, is obtained when form considers the forces that are working on it. It is only when man has ignored the environment and has been cut off from nature that problems arise. We must not distort any of the forces in nature."

He not only recognized and was answerable to the dictates of the environment, but also was able to identify and give meaning to the critical connection between an appropriate design response to natural forces and human needs. He saw that this connection, in turn, has been a key factor in the different architectural expressions of various cultures, and has provided a valuable clue to the meaningful continuation of regional differences.

51

Instead of responding to his plea to reflect environmental and cultural variations in their work, most architects continue to indulge in the same kind of self-serving individualism that characterized the beginnings of the Modern Movement, with its several cults of personality. The profession today, however, is also confounded by a wave of pluralism that seems to be an adjunct to the refraction that has beset all other aspects of contemporary life, resulting in a bewildering kaleidoscope of styles that now answer to fashion rather than the physical and spiritual needs of the people they are intended to serve. Upon close examination, each of these styles is as exclusive, unresponsive and dogmatic in its own way as the Modern Movement was in the past.

As the 20th century draws to a close, it has become very clear that technology, which held such promise at the beginning of the industrial age nearly a century ago, cannot solve every problem and has instead produced many of its own. The legacy of science has ironically been an endangered world, not a better one, and as public awareness of this sobering truth has spread, the entire concept of "progress" has changed as well.

Hassan Fathy offered a world view that is built around a core of humanity rather than abstraction, and on a basis of perpetual renewal, rather than destruction. In answer to the now fashionable cry that "tough times demand tough architecture", his approach shows that tough times, instead, call for kind architecture, and that the human will can prevail. For him the continuity of life, and the tangible manifestations of the most durable values that manage to emerge out of common experience, were far more important than personal recognition. His extreme sensitivity to the lessons of the past also made him keenly aware of the fact that such expression, at its best, has inevitably taken more than one lifetime to complete. When considered in this way, his work was only a part of a cyclical process that must be left to others who follow after him to fulfil. His basic humanity, and belief in meaningful continuity, as well as the selflessness with which he incorporated each of these into his architecture, give his ideas great appeal when they are compared to the confusion, superficiality and egotism that we see around us today, because tradition,

by definition, never goes out of style. If these ideas are ever to prevail, however, his work, in its entirety, must be made available to a wider audience, in order that past misunderstandings may be corrected, and the broad scope of what he has achieved can be appreciated. As can be seen here, his writings went far beyond New Gourna and *Architecture for the Poor*, for which he was most widely known. As important as those two legacies are, they have tended to attach a label to him in the public eye, and to limit an awareness of the many other facets of this complicated, brilliant man. Solving the housing problems of those whom he called the "economic untouchables" of the world, was a concern throughout his life, but his interests ranged far wider than rural, self-help projects.

One of Fathy's most prominent disciples, who has also tasted his share of approbation and critical acclaim, once pinned up a verse from the Holy Qur'an next to a short obituary of Hassan Fathy taken from a Cairo newspaper. The obituary reflected the dismissive attitude that Fathy constantly had to endure in his own country. While this will soon be forgotten, the Sura next to it may be considered a more fitting testimonial. It reads:

"Among the Believers are men
Who have been true to
their covenant with God.
Of them, some have completed
their vow to the utmost
and some still wait.
But they have each never changed
their determination in the least."

Sura xxxiii, 22-24

Hassan Fathy
CONTEMPORANEITY IN THE CITY

It would be valuable to discuss the notion of contemporaneity as it applies to the city. I have stressed the importance of our concepts of time, becoming, and the goal of life in this regard, describing the concept of time as a scale by which city development should be measured, and showing how the discontinuous, hierarchical, growth of human settlements is analogous to nature's pattern of evolution. From this it follows that at any stage of a city's growth we should be able to see if any one element is lagging behind the others in development, as far as we can judge with our total knowledge to date.

If we find such an element, there are two possibilities. Either the lag is due to a human failing, such as ignorance or deliberate malice, in which case we must condemn the element concerned as anachronistic; or, although our judgment shows the element to be anachronistic, if there are other factors, either economic or technological that absolutely forbid its being brought into line with the rest, we have to accept the lag as inevitable. This leads us to the conclusion that there are two kinds of anachronism. One is the visible and flagrant anachronism about which there is no doubt and no argument. The other seems to be anachronistic, but proves to be contemporary from the viewpoint of time. As an example, take Mexico City, which, in spite of its millions of inhabitants, has been described by Professor Mayorga as an agglomeration of communities. We can see that this city is hopelessly anachronistic - as indeed is almost any existing city. The same is true of Cairo, for example, which is a group of juxtaposed administrative districts without a centre giving that conceptual unity which might make the whole something more than the sum of its parts. In fact, all the juxtaposition adds are increased congestion, discomfort in dwelling, circulation and function, premature obsolescence of buildings and unstable land values caused by the faulty configuration and lack of provision in the design for a growing unity of concept.

Yet these cities, like most existing ones, have grown over a long period, and carry the weight of their past with them. The past is past and we cannot change it; therefore it is not anachronistic in this sense of the word. But once we come to improve the city, we accept responsibility for the future; if we try to renew the city plot by plot, we shall not have enough freedom to make it contemporary, whereas if we take it sector by sector, we immediately have the opportunity - and responsibility - of making the sector contemporary. If we fall short, then our work will be anachronistic in both ways, and justly condemned. However, even if we succeed in satisfying the conditions of contemporaneity within the sector, we shall still be left with the whole city, with all of its problems.

Thus it will take a considerable time from the moment when a comprehensive and dynamic town-plan is adopted to make the city wholly contemporary.

Let us consider in more detail what is meant by contemporaneity and anachronism in architecture. I choose architecture because this is the flesh, as it were, of the city. The plan, the lay-out becomes visible only through the actual buildings, and it is in those buildings that the effects of contemporaneity or anachronism will first be apparent. They must be truly relevant to their time and situation, or the city will not be viable in the future.

First I must point out that there are various ways of using the word "contemporary". The dictionary defines it as an adjective meaning "existing, living, occurring at the same time as...". By this definition the word implies a comparison between at least two things, and carries no hint of approval or disapproval, no value-judgment. A correct use of it in this way would be "Napoleon was contemporary with Wellington". But as used by many architects the word does carry a value-judgment. It means something like "relevant to its time", and hence, of course, to be approved of, while conversely "anachronistic" would mean "irrelevant to its time", and is a term of disapproval.

These are good definitions, but raise the twin questions of what we mean by relevance and what we mean by time. Time I have defined. May I emphasize again that settlements each have their own time-scale, and that they develop by stages. In just the same way human knowledge advances in time by successive stages of maturity, and no stage can be omitted nor attained before it is due. (A particularly good example of this timing of revelation is the succession of prophets, from Adam to Christ to Mohammed, each one with a particular mission, each marking an epoch and a stage in the spiritual and cultural development of the race.) Now, if we are to reconcile time with the architects' definition of contemporaneity, we must say that to be "relevant to its time" - to be "contemporary" - a work of architecture must fulfil these conditions: it must be part of the bustle and turmoil, the ebb and flow of everyday life; it must be related harmoniously to the rhythm of the universe; and it must be consonant with man's current stage of knowledge of change. This, it will be seen, is a wide and comprehensive definition of contemporaneity. I feel it is necessary, though, because of certain prevalent misconceptions about what is "contemporary".

In Western Europe, a few decades ago, a periodic and inevitable change occurred in architecture. The architect found that the Classicism of the past had degenerated into Rococo and Art Nouveau, with all that that meant in terms of superficiality and meaningless overdecoration. The architectural imagination seemed stuck in empty formalism.

The first reaction among more progressive architects was to go to the opposite extreme of great simplicity. It so happened that at this time new discoveries and techniques in engineering, and particularly the introduction of reinforced concrete and steel, provided the architect with the means to break away from earlier forms, which was seized in the name of functionalism.

But as architectural movements do not develop overnight, the functionalist soon found that this direction impoverished the imagination and therefore tried to create new rules and find new means of expression. Unfortunately, consciously or unconsciously, perhaps due to limited perception, architects restricted themselves to the use of new engineering techniques which, although they offered new opportunities, did not provide easy answers to the problems of aesthetics on which they had been concentrating.

So some architects went to the work of modern painters and sculptors (which had preceded modern architecture in breaking with the past and creating new forms) and tried to apply the same visual ideas, especially those of the Cubists, to architecture. But all they managed to do was to create new clichés; we can enumerate many features that have become the modern equivalents of the column and cornice. Certainly a few architects did succeed, in certain places, in creating truly contemporary designs, but the majority failed to meet the challenge. A careful survey of what is being done at present in almost all the countries of the world would give a depressingly low statistical average of contemporaneity, for the greater part of the work is anachronistic or irrelevant to architecture.

With few exceptions, architects forgot, in their anxiety to find a new visual idiom, that architecture differs from the other plastic arts and from simple engineering, both in its canons as an art in its own right, and in it social implications and relationship to humans.

Thus architects who adopted this attitude, in reaction against the admittedly false architecture of the Rococo and Art Nouveau, found themselves still stuck in sterile formalism, even though they had changed the form.

Some groups of architects and institutions have tried to remedy this by differentiating "modern" from "contemporary", but this change of name has brought about no change of practice, and functionalism still fails to satisfy function in its widest meaning. "Contemporary" architecture in this sense has used the freedom given by new engineering principles to vary the relative sizes of elements in search of visual interest. There is no essential difference between this aesthetic and the classic aesthetic which tried to satisfy the eye by arranging supporting and supported elements. The discoveries of engineers have merely enabled the architect to produce unexpected and strange-looking arrangements that violate our long-acquired sense of proportion, which is based upon our physical strength and instinctive sense of the action of physical forces.

In attacking what passes for contemporaneity in architecture today, I am most emphatically not asking architecture to regress. I respect the work of the masters of the past, but I do not want to arrest architecture in some past century. Indeed, change is a necessary condition of life. It is not innovation that I am against; innovation is neutral, and the architect makes it good or bad. Above all, as I hope I have made clear, I am not condemning contemporaneity, but defending it against the bad name it has acquired. I want to purify the concept of contemporaneity from the incidental and the temporal, to free it from association with particular clichés, and to give the word its noblest significance. For all great architecture is contemporary - of its time, relevant to its situation in space, time and human society - but also eternal. Without being eternal - that is in harmony with the cosmos and the evolution of life - no architecture can be called contemporary. In this sense there is an absolute contradiction between "contemporary" and "ephemeral", which we ought to remember.

The ancient temple builders knew the meaning of contemporaneity. They gave their temples the proportions of the cosmos, and they planned to allow for changes in the order of the heavenly bodies. Even the stages in the growth of the temples were planned so that its proportions would be consonant with those of a growing urban microcosm, as at Luxor. This is exactly the principle we should employ, allowing buildings to follow more than one theme.

I find it very sad that some of the most respected and widely-known architects today choose the ephemeral rather than the contemporary. Like students at architectural schools, they compete with one another in meaningless novelty, for whatever is striking, whatever will earn the applause of the ignorant. They wilfully discard the accumulated experience of centuries, the plain, simple and proven truths not only of aesthetics but of technology as applied to domestic comfort too. They take certain architectural elements whose size and shape have been constant for generations, refined by centuries of trial and error, and which are perfectly adapted to their function, and then, in search of a reputation for originality, distort and misplace them in ways that outrage both common sense and architectural efficiency. For example, they take the simple and useful Venetian blind, enlarge it to enormous proportions, make it in concrete that will not fold away and call it a *brise-soleil*, now mandatory on all "contemporary" buildings. Or they take the Arab *mushrabeya*, which because of the size of its openings and the rounding of its woodwork, softens the light very beautifully, and they inflate this, petrify it, put it outside a plate-glass window, and there you have a *claustra*, which neither permits a view nor softens the light. On the contrary, its hard contrasts of black shadow and brilliant light, produced by the large size of the solid elements and the interstices, dazzle you even more than a plain window would. Not content with the ordinary *claustra*, they enlarge the pattern still further, make it into a wall covering on one side of a London square, and call the result a "contemporary" embassy. Embassies, in fact, seem to excite architects into the most frenetic scramble for novelty as we see here in Athens where there is one which is upside-down - that is, the rooms in it are hung from the roof, though the roof itself is, disappointingly, supported on foundations in the earth. This is a shamefaced surrender to conventionality, attributable to a simple lack of technological imagination, for the architect could easily have suspended the whole embassy from a balloon and tethered it to the ground. It would thus be held *down*, by members in tension, dispensing altogether with old-fashioned compression members that merely hold a building *up*.

Let me firmly define the interpretations of contemporaneity that seem to me to have real meaning. Contemporaneity in planning means consonance with the current stage of change in knowledge and science. Consonance, that is, with humanity's total knowledge of science, which includes our knowledge of the current psychological state of the mass of humanity, and our knowledge of the disciplines relevant to planning - both those the planner should be familiar with and those familiar to the political authority responsible for the plan. Thus contemporaneity is intimately linked with the notion of change. Obviously to be contemporary now means to be wholly relevant to the present. But the "present" is an instant, always changing, and always with us. In the ever-changing social configuration, contemporaneity occurs when the actual configuration coincides with the optimum configuration for the time being. There is, for a given city at any given instant, a cluster of optimum configurations for the various aspects of that city, which together constitute an ideal. A contemporary city is the one in which the reality coincides with the ideal.

I hope I have shown that the meaning of "contemporaneity" that I favour is far subtler and more satisfying than this hastily made combination of visual and engineering aspects, which ignores all the other disciplines that have a bearing on architecture and human settlements: biology, physiology, physics, psychology, economics, sociology, social anthropology, aerodynamics, mechanics and so on. Architecture deals with human beings and buildings, not just buildings. Therefore contemporaneity should apply to both in their inseparable relationship, which necessarily involves all the above studies. If a work of architecture falls short in any one of these respects, and fails to make the best use of the discipline in question, it will be anachronistic - not exploiting to the maximum our present knowledge. For example, if the architect does not take into account the problems of solar radiation or ventilation in house or city planning, or fails to allow for the psychological effect of the quality and absolute size of space or architectural elements, or of the texture of materials and quality of light, then he is wilfully ignoring available knowledge, failing to be contemporary.

There are many cities and parts of cities, old and new, being planned today, all over the world. Yet there is a serious lack of understanding among the planners of the knowledge needed to make these cities contemporary. (Indeed, in very many cases, especially in Africa, there is a serious lack of planners, but this is another matter.) In our setting out of the problems confronting what cities should be like in the future, the state of dissemination of knowledge deserves a section to itself. In planning a new city, or in forecasting, the knowledge or lack of knowledge among planners is a most important factor, and must be taken into account. Their responsibility starts from the moment when they are informed.

What sort of information do we consider planners must have to be effective? They need to understand the problem of human settlements in its totality, and to realize the wide range of sciences that must be consulted in making any sort of planning decision. Almost all planning faults are faults of partiality, of not being comprehensive enough or not being thorough enough.

Architecture concerns human beings and buildings; planning concerns human beings, society and buildings.

An existing town changes the greater part of its buildings every fifty years, more or less. Some, such as Mexico City, change them even more quickly. But although the totality of buildings has been renovated, the share of the city does not change. It is rather like the human body, which is said to change every single cell within seven years, but which does not change its shape, in spite of this. Thus, streets and plots remain the same. Even after the opportunity created by the Great Fire of 1666, London was rebuilt on its old inconvenient plan, simply because the plots remained the same; so that today the City of London follows a 400 year-old street plan. Thus, even though the individual buildings of a city may be 100% contemporary, this contemporaneity stops short at the private plot, and cannot be carried up through the hierarchy of sectors. Even when a city spreads and builds on new land, its contemporaneity will be limited by the size of possible sectors and the possibility of integrating those sectors into a dynamic and organic growth.

The wholly contemporary design is in no way anachronistic. Anachronism can be precisely measured. It is well-known that any building in which thermal capacity is unnecessarily large, and in which the consequent load on the heating system is unduly high, is considered old-fashioned by American insurance companies, who will not insure such a house because it is uneconomical to run and hence difficult to sell. In such a case the degree of anachronism of this building, from the point of view of physical science, may be expressed in the number of BTUs or kilocalories in excess of the economic ratio (building/heat) needed to bring the building up to the required temperature. The architect has failed to apply existing knowledge, and should brush up on physics.

On the other hand, a glass-walled house in, say, Lagos (or Paris, for that matter), that needs more power to cool it than the economic ratio (building/heat) would suggest, is anachronistic in this respect by the amount of excess power, or by the BTUs to be expelled. Again, the architect who builds a sort of solar furnace and then brings in a vast refrigerating plant to make it habitable is over-simplifying the problem and is working below the level of architecture.

In a similar way, if the various blocks in a sector are implanted in such a way that air movement through and around these blocks is unnecessarily impeded - if the architect has not consulted the findings of aerodynamics - then the lay-out is anachronistic and the anachronism, with respect to physiology, can be stated as the difference between the optimum thermal comfort and the attained thermal comfort, while with respect to aerodynamics it can be stated as the difference between the optimum air movement and the attained air movement. Similar measures of anachronism may be obtained with respect to economics, technology and various other relevant sciences.

All this is not to say that designs can be *created* by science, but simply that design requires that a certain minimum of scientific knowledge be applied. Within the fields to which science is applicable, the degree of application can be measured, and thus provides a check on the contemporaneity of the design.

The above article, which was prepared for the Athens Center of Ekistics, is part of the "City of the Future" project carried out there in 1961, to which Hassan Fathy contributed an extensive analysis.

Arif Hasan
THE SEARCH FOR A SOCIALLY RESPONSIVE ARCHITECTURE

In the last century massive social, political and demographic changes have taken place in the Islamic World due to colonial occupation, the industrial revolution and its global repercussions, and the nature and aspirations of the post-World War II liberation movements and their geo-political alignments. These changes had a two-fold effect on the built environment in Islamic countries. In rural areas they destroyed the traditional structure of society and along with it the hereditary artisanal tradition and the services sector which built and managed the rural and, in many cases, the urban built environment as well. In addition, they led to the commercial exploitation of community lands and resources, the main source for traditional building materials and land for the expansion of settlements. These repercussions, in turn, have led to the non-availability of traditional building materials and affordable skills, leading to a major decline in the quality of the built environment. More often than not they have also led to homelessness and marginalisation of entire communities.

On the other hand the changes of the last century have led to large-scale urbanization, mainly due to rural-urban migration of poor and destitute families, in search of a better future. This process of urbanization is a powerful Third World phenomenon of which the Islamic World is very much a part. Urban growth in most major cities of the Third World in the sixties and seventies has ranged from 4% to 7.5% per year. Furthermore, it is estimated that whereas, between 1980 and 2000, the number of poor rural households in Third World countries will decline from 80 to 58 million, the number of poor urban households will increase from 40 to 74 million. During this period the population of the Muslim World will increase from 800 million to 1400 million, and most of it will be squeezed into the major urban centres of the Islamic World such as Jakarta, Dhaka, Karachi, Tehran and Cairo.

Islamic and other Third World governments and professionals have not been able to respond to the problems posed by the pace and scale of this urbanization, nor to the problems generated in the rural areas. This is because most of these countries have a poor resource base, low income per capita and high population growth rates. As such, the vast majority of their populations cannot afford the cost of formal conventional development. In addition, the state often does not have the financial, managerial or technical resources to effectively plan and subsidize this development, or to subsequently operate and maintain it properly.

The problem is further compounded by the adoption by Muslim countries of inappropriate First and Second World institutional and development models, that are capital intensive, do not make use of the immense human and entrepreneurial resources that Third World communities possess, and are incompatible with the sociology and economics of low-income groups whose problems and settlements dominate the urban scene.

The failure of the state and the formal sector to effectively address the physical and social requirements that the changes of the last century have created has led to massive degradation of the built environment. In the absence of planned expansion for the increasing economic activities in the city, old city centres have been turned into wholesale markets, warehousing and sweat shops, and in the process their architectural and cultural heritage has either been destroyed and replaced by substandard utilitarian buildings, or is in a state of advanced decay. Densification has eliminated parks, open spaces and formal *maidans*, over-taxed the existing infrastructure and created ad-hoc additions to the houses in the old residential districts, destroying both their physical and social fabric. Many historic cities of the Islamic World are increasingly dominated by an unregulated transport sector serving the new functions that have evolved in them, and have ceased to cater to human beings.

The failure to provide affordable housing for the urban poor has led to the development of informal settlements in almost all major cities of the Muslim World. Most of these are squatter settlements on government land; many are in ecologically unsafe areas prone to seasonal flooding, along railway tracks or in old quarries; others are unplanned, often illegal, subdivisions of valuable agricultural land; and yet others are rentals on private land, managed by powerful mafias and toughs. In almost all cases these settlements have little or no physical infrastructure or social amenities, and their residents have no *de jure* security of tenure.

In the sixties and seventies, the response of Islamic governments and professionals to these major problems was based primarily on First and Second World models. At state expense, restoration of historic monuments in the old city centres was undertaken, but little could be done, due to a lack of resources, to rehabilitate the degraded neighbourhoods and districts around them. Later, attempts at conservation were made, but in the absence of community involvement and due to financial constraints, they remained small islands in a stormy sea of uncontrolled development, and refused to grow.

The state also undertook to provide housing and social facilities for increasing urban populations. High-rise flats, community buildings, schools and clinics in the International Style cropped up in major Islamic cities. Most of these buildings were climatically and culturally unsuitable and socially unacceptable to the users. In addition, due to their high costs, the users could not pay for them, and the state could not produce them on a sufficiently large scale to overcome even a small fraction of the problems or large-scale rapid urbanization. By the mid-seventies it was obvious that the "solution" of the state as a "provider" had failed.

In this period the state was so obsessed by building new townships complete with all social amenities that it failed to cater to the social and recreational needs of the other parts of the city where the social fabric was being destroyed by unregulated land use changes and densi-fication. The section of the population most affected in this regard has been children and the youth who were forced to play in the congested and polluted streets.

By the early seventies a number of Third World architects and planners had rejected the conventional model of development and the architecture it produced. They insisted that the state could not deliver if its role continued to be that of a "provider". They insisted that architecture and planning should be compatible with the culture and sociology of the people it was meant for, and that it was not the job of the architect to create new "life styles" that reflected what was unilaterally

ABOVE: East Wahdat Upgrading Programme - the community prior to improvement; Sidharth Colony, Bandara East, Bombay, India; Moquattam Zabbaleen Community Improvement, Cairo, before intervention.

conceived by him to be the "spirit of the age". They insisted that only low-cost and economic solutions could tackle the scale of urban growth and rural decay in the Third World and that in searching for these solutions, the role of technology would have to be subservient to social conditions and development processes and procedures. They promoted the use of local materials for building and the revival of old technologies and the development of new ones to make this possible. They argued that even if these technologies were not cheaper, they benefitted the local economies. They challenged conventional standards and supported the idea of incremental development. To support their contentions and proposals they pointed to the role of communities and the informal sector in providing land, social amenities, housing and jobs to low-income settlements. They pointed out that in terms of both scale and financial investment, the contribution of the state to physical and economic development of Third World urban centres was just a small fraction of what the poor had contributed, and that these two forms of development must complement each other. In addition, they pointed out that the architecture of informal settlements, though substandard both in design and technology, was human in scale, conducive to the development of social interaction, and compatible with the culture of its residents.

Out of these contentions were born a number of principles which have slowly come to dominate the thinking of an increasing number of architects and planners in the Islamic World. Within this group it is felt that solutions on a large enough scale to be effective can only be achieved if the state and professionals can support the communities in tackling their own problems by raising their awareness levels, mobilising their resources, providing them with technical support, and making them partners in planning and development. Out of this was born the concept of the professional or state as a "facilitator" rather than a provider. In addition, it was felt that the maximum benefit for the largest number should be achieved through the minimum financial investment, and that costs and processes of management and maintenance should be sustainable.

In concrete terms these concepts led to the

FROM ABOVE: East Wahdat Upgrading Programme - the community in its surrounding fabric after improvement; Tara Housing Project, Architect: Charles Correa; The Kampung Improvement Programme, Jakarta, Architects: K.I.P. Technical Unit.

development of a number of new approaches. Restoration and state-promoted conservation projects were replaced by ones in which people participated and the restored and renovated areas became places of recreation and cultural activity for the city, rather than museums and monuments. In addition, their conservation, management and maintenance became the responsibility of local governments and communities rather than that of the departments of antiquity or archaeology. In architecture too, there was a search for historic and cultural continuity and designs that were environmentally appropriate.

Public housing, often on land vacated by bulldozed squatter settlements, was replaced by projects aimed at regularising and upgrading informal settlements. To facilitate this process a variety of innovative credit, design and technical support systems were created. Upgrading of settlements also led to the creation of open spaces and the attention of planners moved to the recreational needs of low-income groups.

Initially these new concepts were not acceptable to state institutions and to the architectural and planning establishments in most Islamic societies, and most of the projects based on them were carried out by a handful of professionals for non-government social welfare organizations. It was only in the latter part of the seventies that some governments agreed to play the role of a "facilitator" through small pilot projects and the professional and academic establishments began to discuss the repercussions of this new approach to architecture and professional education. This discussion still continues.

In the initial stages this new approach failed to meet its objectives. Up to the mid-eighties, if a project was sound as an architectural and physical planning exercise, it failed to meet its social and economic objectives and hence the criteria of sustainability and replicability. If, on the other hand, it was sustainable, replicable and socially responsible, it was very often of poor architectural quality.

The Aga Khan Award for Architecture premiated a number of such projects in its previous four cycles, such as the Kampung Improvement Programme in Jakarta in 1980, the Hafsia Quarter Upgrading in 1983, the Conservation of the Mostar Old Town in 1986 and the Grameen Bank in 1989. However, in all these cycles the overwhelming majority of the premiated projects were far removed from the principles of the state or the professional as "facilitator" or "maximum benefit for the largest number through minimum financial investment", and few could be termed as environmentally "appropriate". In addition, even in a number of projects where these principles were reflected, the jury expressed its concern that either quality had not been met or the criteria of sustainability and replicability had been sacrificed.

In this cycle of the Award all the premiated projects respond to the social, economic and cultural needs of Islamic societies. They are replicable and sustainable and the purely architectural ones use local materials and technologies and indigenous forms. And they are of a high architectural and planning quality and all are the work of local architects. It seems that the movement of the early seventies against what was considered as an "inappropriate" response to the needs of contemporary Islamic societies, has at last come of age.

TOP ROW, LEFT TO RIGHT:
Ronald Lewcock, Fumihiko Maki, Renata Holod, Frank
Gehry, Charles Moore, Suha Özkan (AKAA), Saïd Zulficar.

MIDDLE ROW:
Mohammed Arkoun, Balkrishna Doshi, His Highness
The Aga Khan, Ismaïl Serageldin.

BOTTOM ROW:
Arif Hasan, Selma al-Radi, John de Monchaux, Ali Shuaibi,
Dogan Tekeli, Adhi Moersid, Muhammad Yunus, Azim
Nanji.

REPORT OF THE 1992 AWARD JURY

In this, the fifth cycle of the Aga Khan Award for Architecture, nine projects have been premiated. They were selected from an initial group of two hundred and fifty-nine nominations and a list of twenty-seven finalists that were visited on-site by a team of eleven technical reviewers. The Jury feels that they have discovered exemplary projects whose essence, directness and modesty have lessons for the world at large. The Jury notes the growth and maturing of cultural and architectural awareness in what hitherto have been regarded as marginal areas. It applauds the successful and imaginative solutions which enhance urban environments. It rejoices in the competence of local professional cadres who have used their architectural and planning skills to create places of dignity and to generate new architectural languages. The premiated projects are viable solutions which address issues of limited and diminishing resources and problems of the underprivileged in decaying neighbourhoods. The Jury believes that these economically sustainable, humanistic solutions are relevant for the developed countries as well as the developing world.

The premiated projects are:

I. **Enhancing Urban Environments**	II. **Generating New Architectural Languages**
Kairouan Conservation Programme Kairouan, Tunisia	Stone Building System Dar'a Province, Syria
Palace Parks Programme Istanbul, Turkey	Demir Holiday Village Bodrum, Turkey
Cultural Park for Children Cairo, Egypt	Panafrican Institute for Development Ouagadougou, Burkina Faso
East Wahdat Upgrading Programme Amman, Jordan	Entrepreneurship Development Institute of India Ahmedabad, India
Kampung Kali Cho-de Yogyakarta, Indonesia	

ENHANCING URBAN ENVIRONMENTS

Kairouan Conservation Programme

Kairouan, Tunisia

Palace Parks Programme

Istanbul, Turkey

Cultural Park for Children

Cairo, Egypt

East Wahdat Upgrading Programme

Amman, Jordan

Kampung Kali Cho-de

Yogyakarta, Indonesia

OPPOSITE: Kampung Kali Cho-de, Yogyakarta, Indonesia.

KAIROUAN REHABILITATION PROGRAMME
KAIROUAN, TUNISIA

Conservators and Planners:
Association de Sauvegarde de la
Médina de Kairouan

Brahim Chabbouh, President
Mourad Rammah, Secretary General
Hedi Ben Lahmar, Restoration
Architect

Completed: 1979 and ongoing

Kairouan was founded in the 7th century by Uqba bin Nafi, a famous commander and close companion of the Prophet. It was the first Arab city in the Maghreb and lies inland approximately 160km south of Carthage on a flat and arid plateau. It became the capital of the Aghlabids in the 9th and 10th centuries when it was transformed into a brilliant town, a centre for research and for the dissemination of knowledge and ideas. During the next centuries, its prosperity diminished and it was not until the 18th century that the town re-established its prestige as well as its commercial prosperity and industrial base.

Today, Kairouan is a *medina* protected by ramparts, with a network of narrow, winding streets, mosques, blind alleys and white-washed buildings, imposing portals, minarets and cupolas. The buildings of this traditional urban town are built almost exclusively of brick, bonded by a lime and earth mortar. The white-washed façades give the town its homogeneous texture.

When the *Association de Sauvegarde de la Médina de Kairouan* (ASM) was established in 1977, the town was in a serious state of neglect. Important monuments were in imminent danger of collapsing or had been converted into makeshift houses. An extensive restoration and rehabilitation programme was initiated, with important monuments taking top priority:

Mosque of Ibn Khayrun
Built in the 9th century, this mosque is a fine example of Aghlabid architecture with a rare carved stone façade. ASM dismantled the front façade stone by stone and rebuilt it after consolidating the foundations. Fissures, cracks and the roof were also repaired.

Khan Barrouta
Built in the 18th century, the two-storeyed *khan* is reached through a stone, arched portal decorated with

Typically, larger structures have been placed at the intersection of streets in the medina, as here, where a high vertical element helps to define space and distance.

69

floral motifs. The building was in such a ruinous condition that it had to be restored one section at a time.

Mosque of Al Bey

Founded by Mohammed Bey in the 17th century, the mosque was built over a covered *suq* and suffered from multiple fissures. It was carefully restored.

Bir Barrouta

Dating back to the founding years of the town, the Barrouta Well (*bir*) was first restored in the 17th century. A two-storeyed building, it is covered by a simple dome on the upper floor. There is room enough for a camel to circle the well so as to draw up the water. It has been completely restored.

Mausoleum of Sidi Khedidi

The mausoleum was built in the 18th century but had become dilapidated and deserted. A unique, double-bent access leads into the single courtyard, prayer hall and funerary chamber, which has a painted ceiling. It was largely rebuilt, and is now used as a school for the deaf.

Mausoleum of Sidi Abid al Ghariani

Built in the 14th century, the tomb consists of a two-storeyed building clustered around three courts. It was the first restoration done by ASM. It had suffered from neglect, so parts of the walls had to be demolished and rebuilt.

Mausoleum of Sidi "Amor" Abada

Popularly known as the "Mosque of the Swords", this building was built in the 19th century and had been recently used as a dispensary. A small part has been restored to function as a crafts museum.

Mausoleum of Sidi Sahib

Dating back to the 7th century, the mausoleum reputedly contains the remains of Abu Jama'a Al-Balawi, one of the companions of the Prophet. A large part of the present building was rebuilt in 1629, the minaret and *madrasa* in 1685, and the whole was greatly restored in the 19th century. The restoration of the large entrance court, the colonnaded vestibule to the mausoleum court and the mausoleum itself is complete, but work on the *madrasa* is still in progress.

Suq of Cisterns

This 14th century market consists of sixty shops lining a street covered by a tunnel vault. It fell out of use in the 1960s but has now been restored as a market.

A variety of materials and styles have been used on the doorways of houses and other buildings, with each design being unique. Layered views through a series of archways to a melon ribbed dome in the distance help to provide scale to the city.

71

Water Basins of the Aghlabids

Built in the 9th century by Abu Ibrahim Ahmad, the larger of the two basins is 128 metres in diameter while the smaller is 37.4 metres in diameter. They have been water-proofed and restored.

Ramparts

The existing walls of Kairouan were built in the 18th century, roughly following the contours of the adobe walls of the 11th century. Foundations have been consolidated, the walls have been restored, and the gates have also been rebuilt.

The rehabilitation and restoration of these important monuments in Kairouan has been carefully accomplished with due respect for their historical qualities. Only traditional and local building techniques and materials have been used. Funds for restoration were obtained only from entrance fees to the monuments. By using unsophisticated technology and simple and available materials, the ASM were able to restore and upgrade not only the monuments of their historic town but also to improve the physical welfare of the people. With the increase of tourism, more jobs are available to the residents.

This enlightened and simple approach to the restoration of a historic town will serve as an inspiration to others.

The Jury praised this project as follows:

The transformation of a passive, protectionist bureaucracy into a concerned and dynamic association for the conservation of the city has ensured, over the last fifteen years, the continued integrity of an historic urban fabric. The programme repaired and restored numerous shrines and religious buildings as well as their dependent spaces and introduced new functions while respecting historic importance and religious significance. More than twelve individual sites have been redeveloped in this fashion to house functions such as a school for deaf children, offices, social services, and crafts centres. The expertise and experience gained in the programme were developed entirely from local initiatives and resources, and are now available to private owners for the repair, upgrading and restoration of their properties. The restored and reactivated sites have become an attraction for visitors as well as providing improved services for the inhabitants of the city. The programme sets an excellent example for adapting an existing urban fabric to contemporary requirements.

Crenellated walls and high, colonnaded gates delineate the boundary of the medina.

74

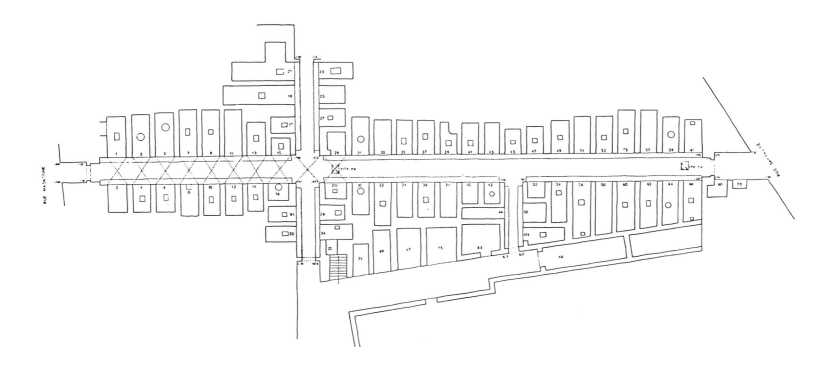

Narrow, tightly spaced streets provide shade, which can significantly lower temperatures during the hottest time of the day. Latticework screens also provide privacy; BELOW: Plan of the Suq of Cisterns.

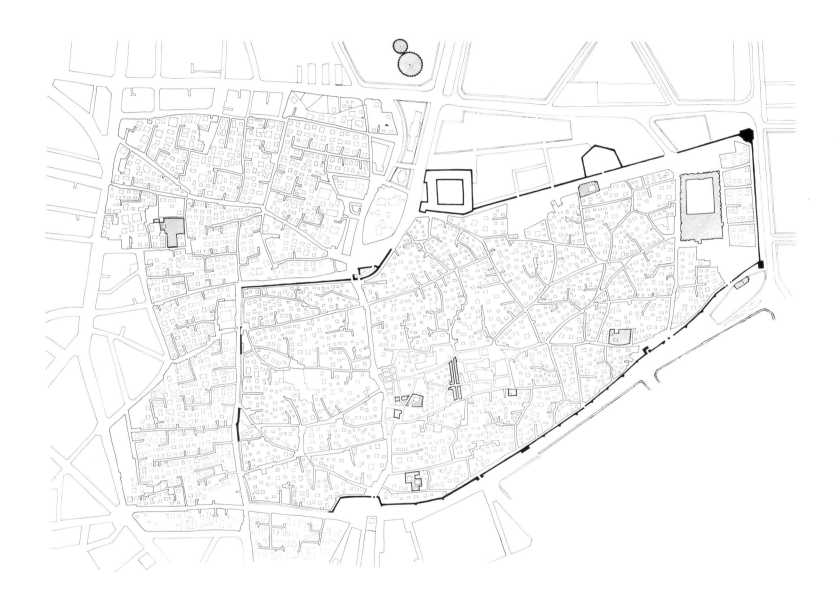

*ABOVE L TO R: The qibla of the Great Mosque of Kairouan;
A detail in the Dar M'Rabet; BELOW: Site plan of Kairouan;
OPPOSITE: The minbar of the Mosque of el Bey (1683),
which is the only Hanefite mosque built by the Ottoman
governor Mohammed Bey.*

ABOVE L AND R: The Ferhat Cemetery; BELOW L TO R: A dome near the water basin; The Water basin; OPPOSITE: The minaret of the Great Mosque of Kairouan.

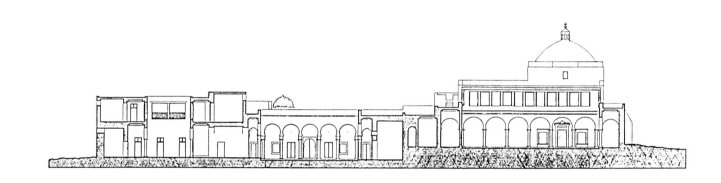

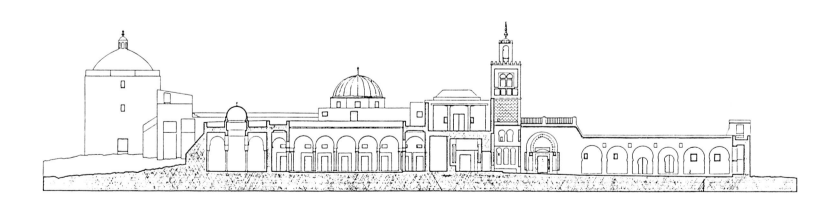

*ABOVE: Formal and informal entrances into Sidi Sabib;
BELOW: Sectional-elevations of the Sidi Sabib Mausoleum;
OPPOSITE: The inner courtyard of the Mausoleum of Sidi
Sabib.*

81

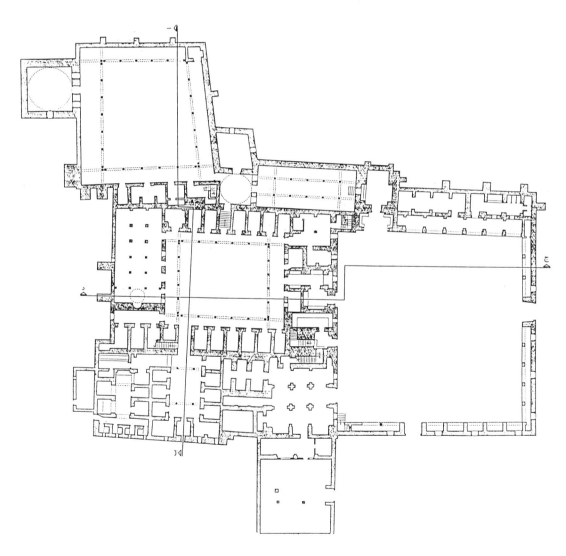

ABOVE: *Looking toward the dome of the Mausoleum of Sidi Sahib; BELOW: Plan of Sidi Sahib; OPPOSITE: Tilework inside an arcade in the Mausoleum of Sidi Sahib.*

84

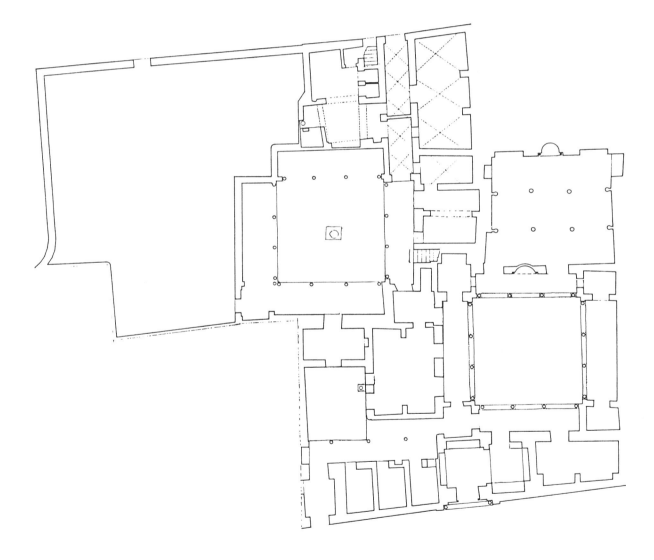

ABOVE: Wall and column details inside the Zaouia of Sidi Abid; BELOW: Plan of the Zaouia of Sidi Abid al Ghariani; OPPOSITE: Courtyard of Sidi Abid.

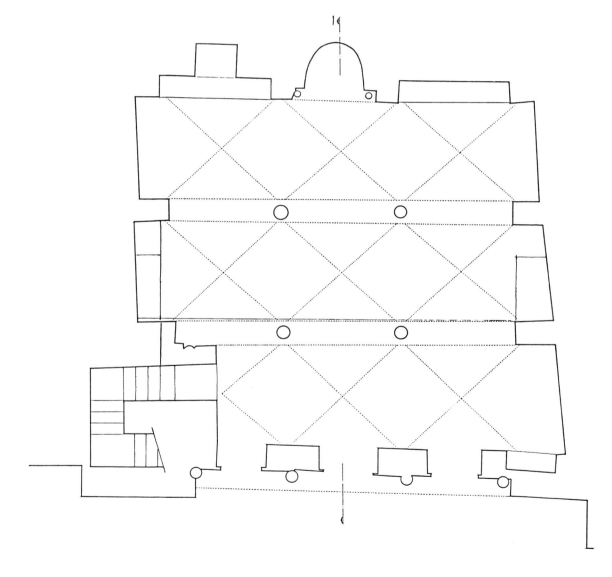

*ABOVE L TO R: The Three Door and Zitouna mosques; BELOW:
Plan of the Ibn Khayrun or "Three Door" mosque; OPPOSITE:
Main entrance of the Okba Mosque.*

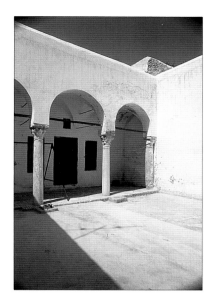

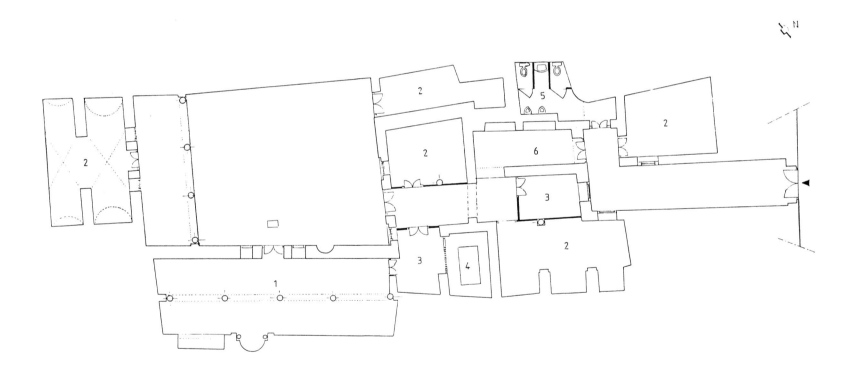

ABOVE L TO R: The 18th Century Mausoleum of Sidi Khedidi and the 19th Century Mausoleum of Sidi Abdelkader; BELOW: Ground floor plan of the Sidi Khedidi Mosque; OPPOSITE: The domes of the Mausoleum of Sidi "Amor" Abada, in the north-western part of the medina, outside the wall.

PALACE PARKS PROGRAMME
ISTANBUL, TURKEY

Conservators and Architects:
Regional Offices of The National
Palaces Trust

Metin Sözen, *Director*

Client: The Turkish Grand National
Assembly

Completed: 1984 and ongoing

In March 1924, the Grand National Assembly of the
Turkish Republic nationalized all the palaces of the
Ottoman Sultans. In 1983, a regional directorate of the
National Palaces Trust (NPT) was created for Istanbul.
The aim of the NPT was to open these buildings to the
public after restoring them and re-assembling their
original furnishings. Each palace was to be provided
with a social function that would attract visitors and
allow the structures to be absorbed into the urban
fabric. Six palace complexes have been opened to the
public since that date. The work continues.

Dolmabahçe Palace
This is the largest and most opulent of the palaces.
Built in 1856 by Sultan Abdülmecit, the Dolmabahçe is
composed of several pavilions and courts including
the men's apartments or *selamlik*, the throne room and
the women's section or *haremlik*. It contains 285
chambers and 46 large halls. Little architectural
restoration work has been undertaken in the main
palace building; decayed elements have been replaced
with pre-cast stone (which may not bode well for the
future), and roofs and walls have been repaired. Most
of what has been done cannot be categorised as
restoration - upkeep and a minimum maintenance
would best describe the work of the NPT. The valuable archival material, which was discovered in the
palace and subsequently used for guiding all of the
restorations, is still kept here. The kitchens and the
store-rooms were converted into exhibition halls, and
the gardens and aviary were restored to their original
splendour. The colours that were used by the Otto-
mans to identify the different sections of the gardens
were re-established: red identifies the administrative
quarters, yellow is used in the aviary and also for the
crown prince's garden, and pink characterizes the
harem gardens.

ABOVE: Typical stone-carving details of the Palace Parks
Programme; OPPOSITE: Map showing the location of the
National Palaces within the cityscape of Istanbul.

Beylerbeyi Palace

This palace was built as a summer residence during the reign of Sultan Abdülaziz (1861-1876) on a 20 acre, terraced site. It is smaller than Dolmabahçe with only 24 rooms and six halls, and has been functioning as a museum for many years, with the most notable pieces being the original furniture designed and built by Sultan Abdülhamit II. By referring to archival material, including old photographs, the NPT successfully re-created the original state and character of the palace. The stables and other pavilions on the grounds were converted into museums or exhibition halls. A 100 metre tunnel that formed part of the imperial route has been restored and now serves as the public entry to the palace.

Aynalikavak Pavilion

This is the earliest among the palaces in the possession of the NPT, dating from the reign of Sultan Ahmet III (1703-1730). It is a small, wooden pavilion with five interconnecting rooms set in a garden overlooking the Golden Horn. It has painted and gilded walls and ceilings; crystal chandeliers add to the sense of opulence.

Maslak Lodges

The Maslak Pavilions were built as hunting lodges during the reign of Sultan Abdülaziz (1861-1876) on the edge of a small woodland. Each one is different: the Pasalar Dairesi baths are built of stone; the Mabeyn-i-Humayun or State Hall is built of brick and stone with a glass conservatory; the Çadir is built of wood; the main Kasr-i-Humayun or Imperial Lodge is a stone and brick structure clad in wood. The pavilions were in poor condition and had to be re-constructed. Modern construction techniques were used. The conservatory was so destroyed that it had to be re-assembled and re-stocked with plants; the Imperial Lodge was cleaned and its ceiling paintings were restored, while the Pasalar Dairesi baths needed drastic repairs. The grounds have been designated as sports areas and are being developed with running tracks and playing fields.

Ihlamur Pavilions

Ihlamur consists of two pavilions, the Ceremonial House and the Court Pavilion, both of which date between 1849-1855. Set in a peaceful, four-acre wooded valley, this landscaped park gets its name from the lime grove that originally occupied the site; lime trees still grow in the gardens. The two pavilions were renewed in 1978. The NPT restored the gardens and opened them to the public. They also successfully transformed the Court Pavilion into a tea-room where local people can enjoy the splendours of their royal historical past.

ABOVE: Dolmabahçe Palace interior; OPPOSITE: Dolmabahçe Palace seen from the Bosphorus.

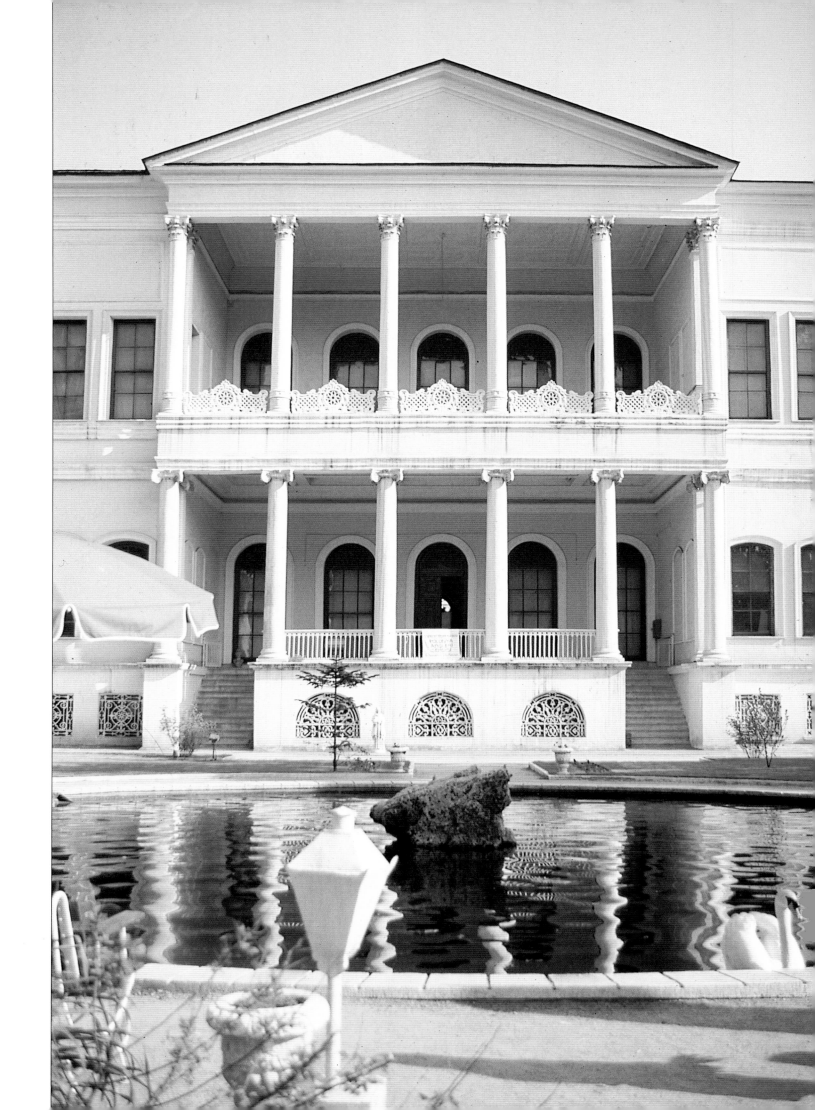

Yildiz Sale

The imperial estates of Yildiz cover an entire hillside in the north-eastern part of Istanbul. Shortly after the accession of Sultan Abdülhamit II (1876-1909), Yildiz became the fourth and final centre of Ottoman administration. The Yildiz Sale and the royal stables were completed between 1889 and 1898. The Sale is maintained by the NPT as a museum guest house with all its Ottoman trappings. The royal stables, on the other hand, have undergone drastic changes in order to turn them into NPT offices and workshops. Since the NPT is a large organization that employs over a thousand people, these alterations threaten to overwhelm the stables.

Although the restoration techniques of the NPT are of uneven calibre, the extraordinary effort that has been put into these palaces preparatory to opening them to the public deserves particular acclaim. By taking up these abandoned and derelict palaces and gardens and turning them into attractive and usable public spaces, the NPT has given back to the people of Istanbul their historical heritage. It has effectively integrated the past into the lively urban present.

The Jury's citation sums it up:

Encompassing eight large parks and more than thirty individual sites, and employing over one thousand individuals, this programme engaged the successful co-operation of academics, government agencies and skilled workers. It represents the active appropriation of an urban heritage by the residents of Istanbul. Spaces and buildings which had remained closed and derelict for decades are now available for public use as places of gathering, entertainment and education. The programme moves beyond the repair and partial restoration of individual palaces and pavilions to the re-building and re-shaping of their dependent buildings and parks. The specialized workshops and training courses of the programme ensure the continuing growth of local expertise in restoration, maintenance, and education. In the increasingly congested cities of the Islamic world, this is a powerful model for the efficient re-use of otherwise undervalued spaces and resources.

ABOVE: Dolmabahçe Palace interior; OPPOSITE: Dolmabahçe Palace.

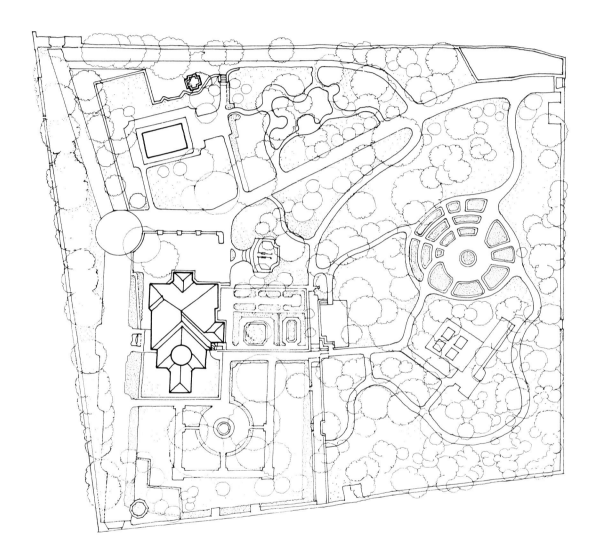

ABOVE: Pavilion interior; BELOW: Site plan of Aynalikavak complex; OPPOSITE: Aynalikavak Pavilion, the oldest of the palaces in the possession of the National Palaces Trust.

ABOVE: Ihlamur Pavilions, Merasim Kosku; BELOW:
Ihlamur Pavilions interior; OPPOSITE: Beylerbeyi (meaning
"the Bey of Beys") Palace, was designed by Serkis Balyan
during the reign of Sultan Abdülaziz (1861-1876).

99

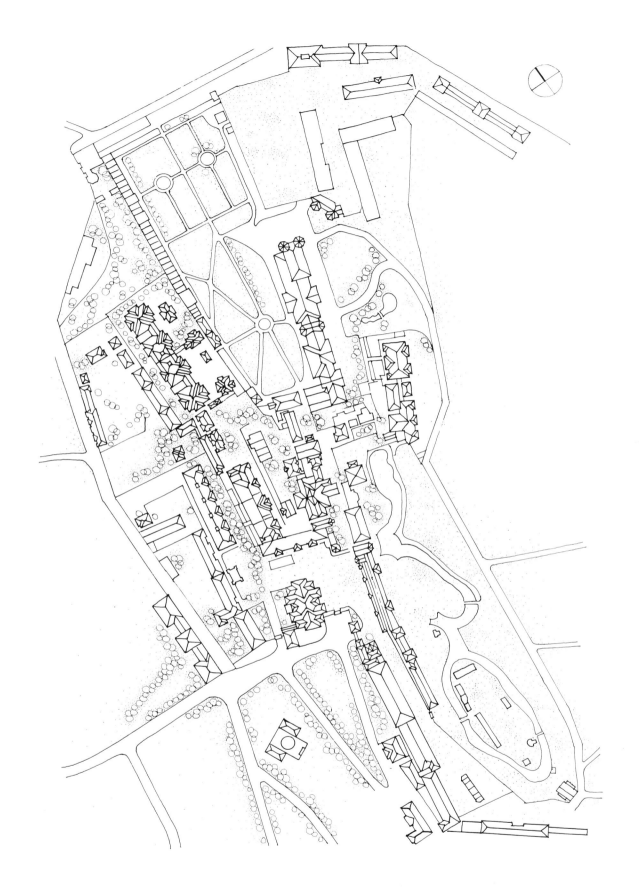

ABOVE: *Plan of Yildiz Sale, with the Büyük Mabeyn and its courtyard enclosure shown at the lower left; OPPOSITE ABOVE: A distinctive feature of the Palace Parks Programme is the establishment of various workshops, including carpentry for restoration; OPPOSITE BELOW: Maslak Lodges.*

The variety of materials used on all the palaces involved in the Palace Parks Programme required the skills of many different craftsmen.

103

CULTURAL PARK FOR CHILDREN
CAIRO, EGYPT

Architect: Abdelhalim Ibrahim Abdelhalim

Client: The Ministry of Culture

Community: The Residents of Abu al-Dahab Neighbourhood

Completed: 1990

The Cultural Park for Children is situated within the old community of Sayyida Zeinab in the heart of medieval Cairo. Spreading over two and a half acres, the park provides libraries, studios, rooms with computer and video games, playgrounds, fountains, and several settings for theatrical and performing arts for this very poor urban community.

The park is laid out in a plethora of complex geometric patterns, some of which are painted in bright colours, to attract the local children. In fact, nearby schools use these patterns to teach the children geometry.

All the users in the neighbourhood, old and young alike, love the project and are proud of it. It has raised the level of their self-confidence. This architectural garden has become an oasis in an otherwise poor and desolate section of Cairo.

The Jury recognizes the approach used by the architect as follows:

The development of this project created a unique space in an otherwise derelict, though historically significant, part of the Cairene cityscape. It resulted in an environment which engages curiosity, fantasy, and play. The forms of the park were generated from the surrounding monuments and demonstrate the governing principles of geometry to children. From the moment of its inception, the project sought to engage the residents of the surrounding neighbourhood in its design and execution. The insertion of the park into this congested urban fabric has gone far beyond the original brief. It has generated a renewed sense of community by extending its presence into the surrounding streets. The residents take pride in their neighbourhood as well as their park.

ABOVE: Children in the neighbourhood love their park and find many ways to use its various spaces; OPPOSITE: Overview of the Cultural Park for Children, Sayyida Zeinab.

106

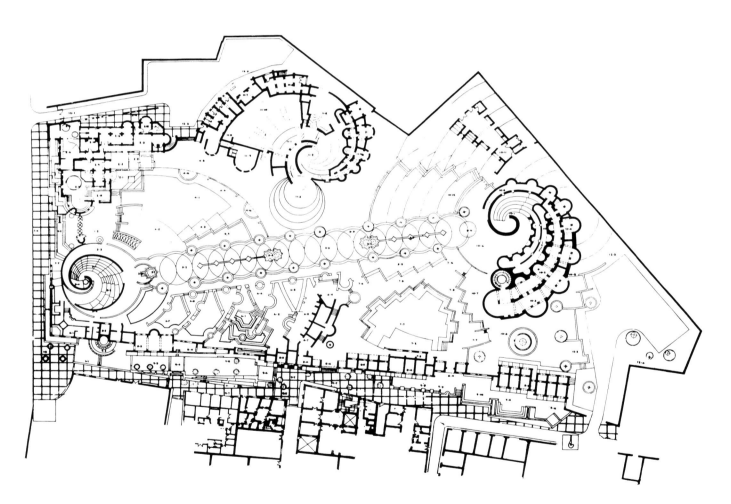

The proximity of the Ibn Tulun Mosque, and other important Mamluk and Ottoman monuments , led the architect to incorporate principles from them into his design. The park is an "intervention " in the truest sense, in that it has dramatically reversed the deterioration that has typified this part of Cairo; BELOW: Site plan of the Cultural Park for Children in Cairo.

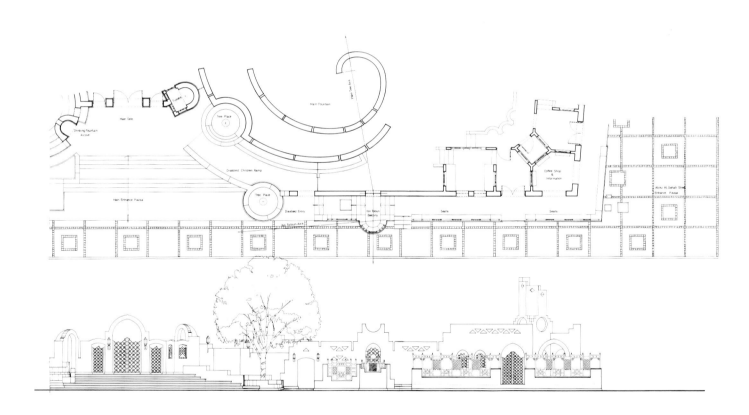

*During the course of construction, changes were made
incrementally, to encourage curiosity and provide delight.
The architectural forms used relate to history, but do not
copy it; BELOW: Main entrance on Kadry Street, part plan
and elevation.*

113

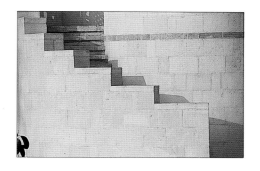

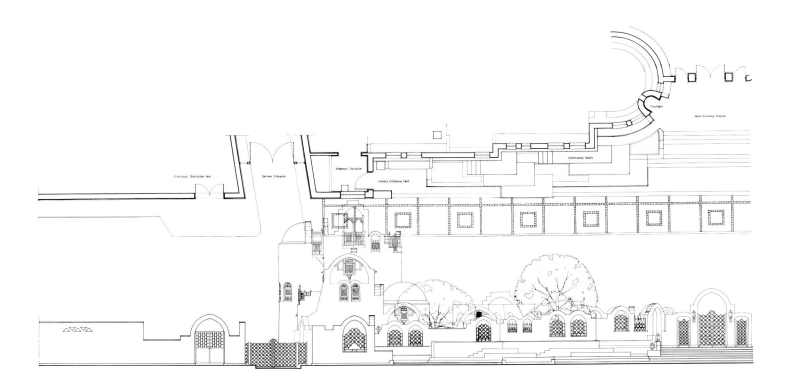

The balance between angular and curved shapes, as abstractions of historical architectural elements that are familiar to the people using the park, is integral to the architect's approach here. The main emphasis of the design is to encourage exploration and empirical learning, through architectural form; BELOW: Continuation of plan and elevation of main entrance along Kadry Street.

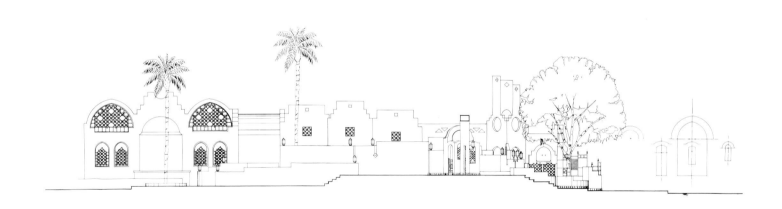

The ways that children use the park do not always conform to preconceptions of how they should react to certain elements, and the architect has tried to provide as much freedom of choice as possible. As architecture and as landscape design, this project is intended to be used, rather than to be simply appreciated as pure, geometrical form; BELOW: Section through main entrance.

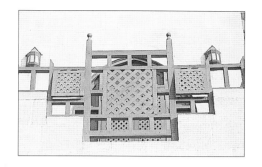

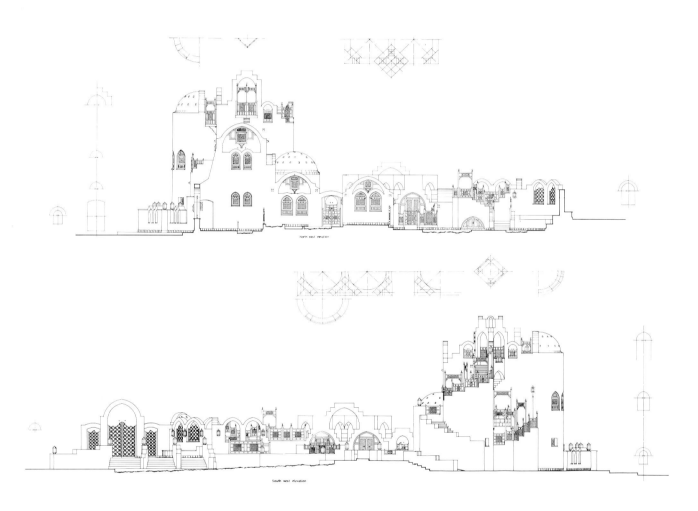

North-east elevation

South-west elevation

*All woodwork has been custom fitted by craftsmen on site to
fit final dimensions. Rooms have also been frequently left
open to the sky, to let the children appreciate the structure
more. The idea of interlocking was one of the four main
principles followed by the architect, and is legible in the
arches here; BELOW: North-east and south-west elevations.*

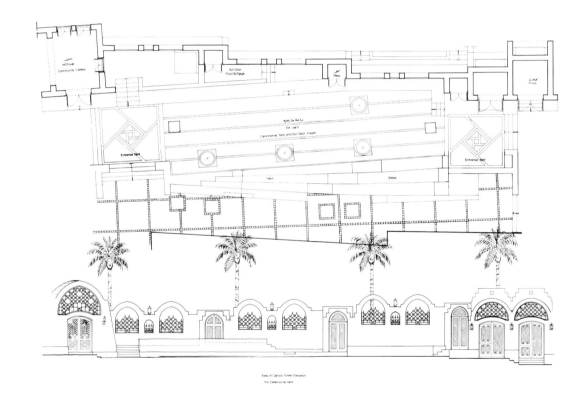

Abou Al-Dahab Street Elevation
The Ceremonial Yard

An important lesson of the Cultural Park for Children is that it is the unsaid, in architecture, which is often the most important thing. Rhythm is a basic theme that unites all the disparate parts of the project, and gives it strength; BELOW: The Ceremonial Yard along Abu al-Dahab Street.

123

EAST WAHDAT UPGRADING PROGRAMME
AMMAN, JORDAN

Planners: Urban Development Department

Yousef Hiasat, Director
Hisham Zagha, Director from 1980-1990
Khalid Jayyousi, Director of Design & Planning
Hidaya Khairi, Director of Population Affairs
Rita Mansour, Design and Layout
Jamal Dali, Social Surveys

Feasibility studies: Halcrow Fox Associates; Jouzy and Partners

Community: The Residents of East Wahdat

Completed: 1980 and ongoing

The East Wahdat Upgrading Programme was begun in 1980 by the Urban Development Department (UDD) of the Government of Jordan. Its aim was to improve the living conditions of residents of informal settlements by enabling them to secure land tenure and by providing them with basic infrastructure, shelter and community facilities. Funds were put together from the World Bank (31%), the Government of Jordan (25%), and the Housing Bank (44%). The land was bought from the original owners and mortgaged to the householders with monthly instalments based on 33% of the income of each beneficiary.

East Wahdat lies in a hilly area just to the north of the Al-Wahdat Refugee Camp. The population of the settlement at the start of the project consisted of about 500 families, almost all of them Palestinian. These refugees had settled on land whose owners had forbidden the construction of permanent shelters; therefore, their houses were made of corrugated iron sheets tacked to wooden frames. There were no services in the settlement, no schools, no health facilities - it was the most abject and under-developed area in Amman.

Today, there are 524 serviced plots with well-built houses as well as 58 shops and 24 workshops that are owned by individuals in the community; 98% of the

The solution to the problems faced by the occupants of East Wahdat has been shown to be directly proportional to the resiliance of the people themselves. In attempting to provide the most basic human needs, of shelter and sanitation, the Urban Development Department has found that uncomplicated means are the most effective.

125

residents have access to water, 96% to sewage mains, and 99% to electricity. By 1985, infant mortality had already fallen from 68 per thousand to 55 per thousand. East Wahdat now has a health centre, a clinic, a mosque, a park and a community centre. It also has surfaced roads and parking spaces.

This amazing transformation was accomplished by the community residents in conjunction with the UDD. Together, they designed each family home.

After upgrading, East Wahdat has all the charming aspects of informal settlements in the Islamic and Third World without the severe environmental problems associated with them. Winding lanes, stepped in places, have no sewage flowing through them. There are small, open places where people can sit, but they are not filled with garbage and mud. The scale of the houses and the open spaces is human.

From a distance, the general appearance of the settlement resembles the piling of hundreds of cubes against the hillside. Up close, however, each house has its own individual character. Each doorway is different, each courtyard has its own dimensions, calligraphic plaques, potted plants and trees, and bright colours identify particular houses. East Wahdat is a place where people live with dignity - it is not a mass housing scheme where the products are identical and anonymous.

The flexible programme that was developed by the UDD, the dedication of the personnel and their interaction with the community, made East Wahdat the success that it is. The process can be easily replicated anywhere in the world.

In the words of the Jury:

Few projects have been able to address a similar range of critical issues during the process of upgrading an urban environment while maintaining a high degree of cost recovery. The project has succeeded in transforming a large squatter population of refugees into proud home owners. The hallmarks of the ten-year programme have been the establishment of suitable building regulations and a physical plan, and the provision of credit without resorting to major state subsidies. The project planners - the Urban Development Department - through their financial and managerial policies have enabled the beneficiary community to create an environment which responds to their social and cultural needs. The autonomy of the department and the dedication of its staff were key factors in the project's success. Except at the initial stage, all technical personnel were locally recruited and have now replicated their expertise and experience gained through this programme in several other sites.

The most common structure used in East Wahdat is the reinforced concrete frame, which is much more durable than the ramshackle sheds of the past - dramatic visual proof of the succession of changes that have taken place in the community.

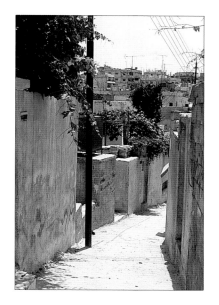

Clean, surfaced walkways have replaced the muddy foot-
paths between houses, helping to raise the self-esteem of the
inhabitants. In its outward appearance, the community now
closely approximates the surrounding urban context of
Amman; BELOW: Proposed upgrading sites in Amman, with
the location of East Wahdat shown at the bottom.

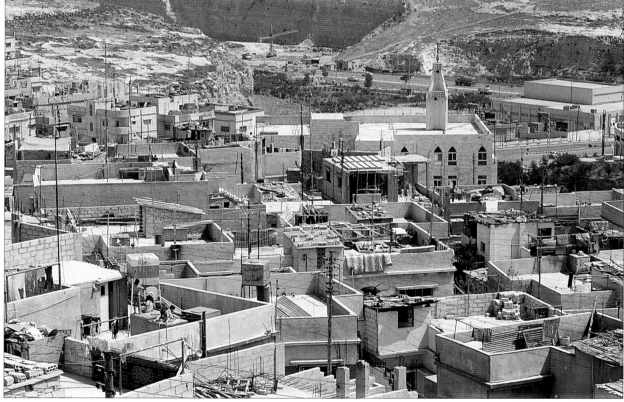

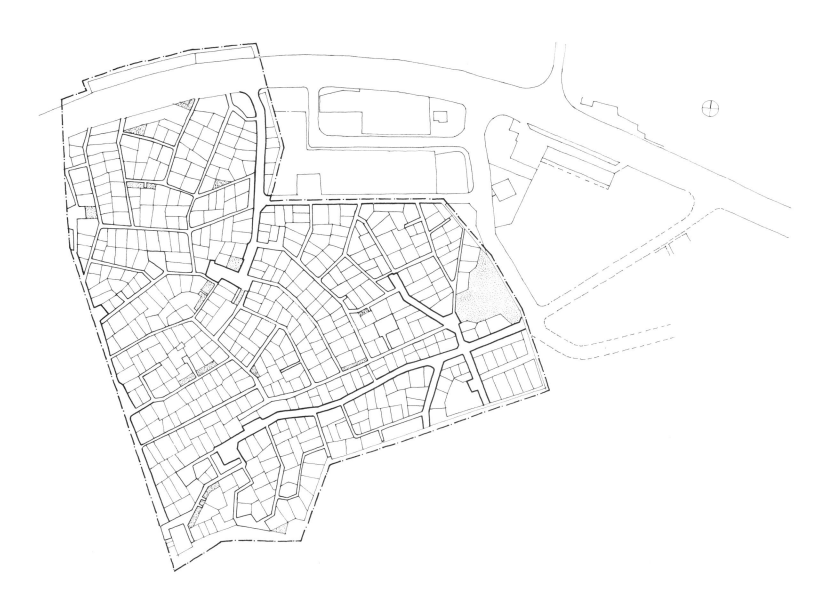

Commercial usage around the fringe of the site, as well as in strategic positions throughout the neighbourhood, was an important part of the financial viability of the project. The choice of materials similar to those being used throughout Amman made sense, since they were readily available; BELOW: Site plan of East Wahdat.

In spite of the size of the site, and the restricted area of individual lots, privacy has been retained to a greater degree than had previously been the case. A series of pedestrian paths serves all parts of the site, and one quarter of the homes have direct access to roads.

135

The individuality of each family is announced by the different design of each doorway. A modular construction system has been used, but people still manage to individualize their dwellings.

The East Wahdat project is replicable, but culturally specific, and has adapted quickly to personalization. Small reminders of the way that the community used to look in the past still remain, but are being replaced.

140

KAMPUNG KALI CHO-DE
YOGYAKARTA, INDONESIA

Architect: Yousef B. Mangunwijaya

Community: Koperasi Permukiman dan Lingkungan Hidup Code Gondolayu

Advisor: Willi Prasetya, Lurah (sector chief)

Artists: Volunteer Art Students in Yogyakarta

Completed: 1985

Kampung Kali Cho-de represents a community which, with the assistance of two key individuals, managed to lift itself from nearly sub-human circumstances to become a neighbourhood of honest - albeit poor - people who are proud of their achievements.

Since the 1950s, Kampung Kali Cho-de has been inhabited by the dregs and outcasts of society. The residents, some 35-40 families, were homeless people from the surrounding countryside who worked at the most menial of tasks. The site is on an extremely steep slope of compacted refuse on the bank of the River Cho-de. The dwellings were made of cartons and plastic sheets which disintegrated with each hard rain.

The development of Kampung Kali Cho-de began in 1973 when Willi Prasetya, the social chief of the area, began his efforts to improve the living conditions of its inhabitants. In 1980, Prasetya asked Y.B. Mangunwijaya, a Catholic priest, to work with the community; in 1983 Mangunwijaya actually moved into the Kampung. These two people convinced the government not to tear down the Kampung and to allow its continued improvement. They also convinced two local newspapers to provide financial help to the Kampung.

The first priority was to build a community centre, "the House of the Brotherhood of Neighbours", where the most needy members - the children - could be taught, and where community issues could be discussed. This centre was built over the edge walls of an existing storm-water sewer, and stone retaining walls were constructed to stop the refuse soil from sliding into the river. Using simple, conical, concrete footings, "A" frame houses were designed and constructed. Bamboo was used for joists and plaited bamboo mats for flooring.

With the help of a group of volunteer art students,

The site of the Kampung is very steeply sloping down to the river Cho-de, making it necessary to build dwellings on raised platforms to fit the topography. The architectural solution provided for Kampung Kali Cho-de is transitory, but effective, efficient and strikingly beautiful.

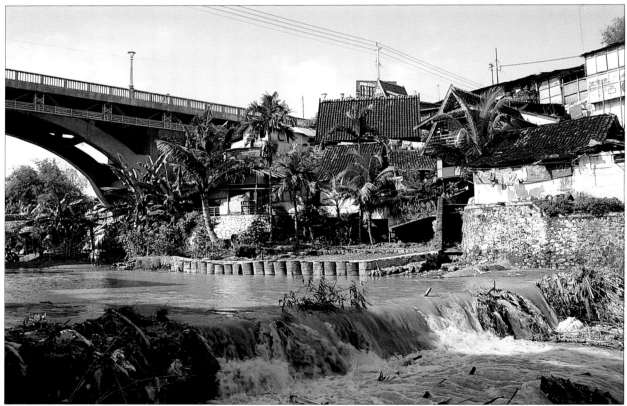

the residents were inspired to paint their houses with colourful decorations. These included stylized patterns and animal and plant motifs, as well as huge monster-like figures. The paintings attracted the attention and interest of tourists, and made the government more tolerant of the formerly illegal settlement.

Building services and site utilities are limited. Drinking and cooking water is supplied by a well near the community centre; the river serves for bathing as well as a latrine. Electricity has been introduced recently for lighting purposes, and payment is made to the co-operative on a wattage basis. There are three televisions.

Prior to its development, Kampung Kali Cho-de was a place of ill-repute that was inhabited by outcasts. Today, it is a peaceful and harmonious community, poor but honest, and proud of its achievement.

The Jury's citation reads as follows:

This small project has accomplished the difficult task of endowing a marginalized population with dignity and self-respect by re-designing a derelict space into an urban environment. It is the result of one man's vision, aided by volunteers, to create a neighbourhood for thirty families who now have homes and the potential for secure, legal status. The architect's skill has yielded a new environment by securing the steep river bank with retaining walls, introducing stilt structures in rural materials, and providing space for a community centre. By the use of decoration and colour, the project achieves a unique vitality and identity. The scale is small, yet the achievement within the given conditions and constraints is immense and humane - a compelling model for the world at large.

Beautiful painted designs add a sense of gaiety to each of the houses. The river, as well as the Gondolayu Bridge to the north, and Faridan M. Noto Street to the east, restrict the project to a long, narrow band along the water's edge.

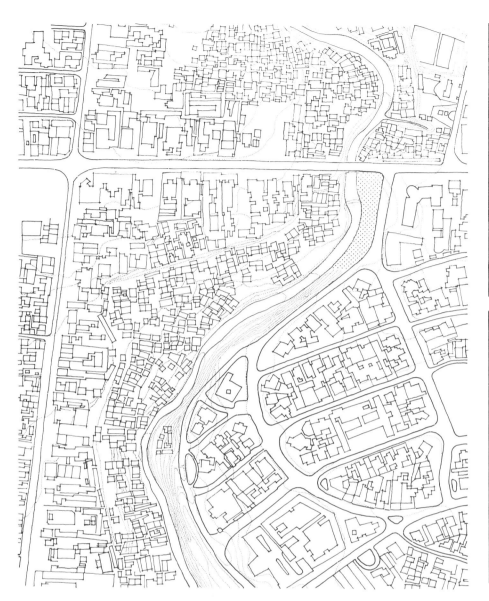

RIGHT: A winding lane twists through the centre of the site; LEFT: Location plan of the project in the neighbourhood; OPPOSITE: Steeply pitched roofs and operable vents high up on the wall help to mitigate the hot, humid and rainy climate in Yogyakarta.

145

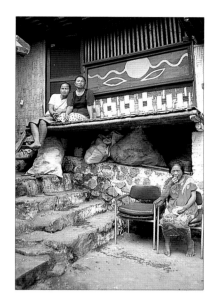

ABOVE : The closeness of the houses and the climate encourage residents to spend much of their time outdoors; BELOW: Site plan; OPPOSITE: The profiles of the houses in the Kampung, which are based on a centuries old rural prototype, blend into their surroundings and are elegant in their simplicity.

147

*Creativity mixed with pragmatism is the hallmark of
Kampung Kali Cho-de; ABOVE L AND R: Water, supplied by
the river, is used for daily needs; BELOW: Schematic section
through the site, and section-elevation.*

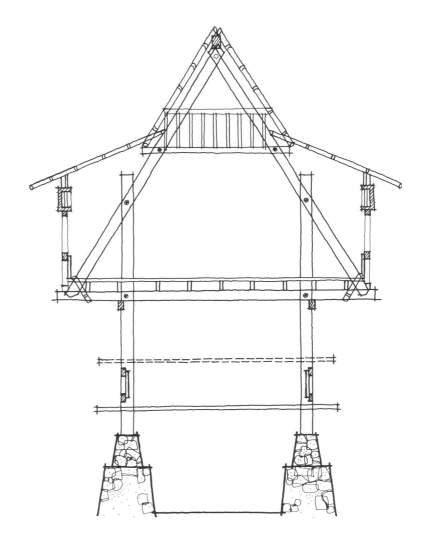

BELOW: Section showing foundations and raised platforms;
OPPOSITE: The Kampung seen from the riverbank.

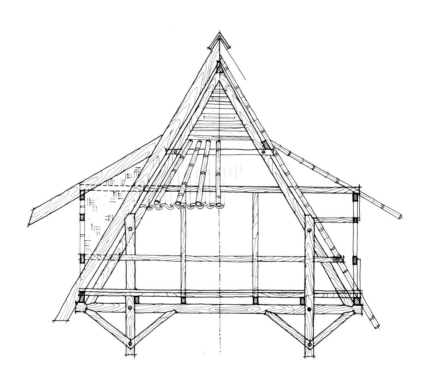

Bright colours and natural materials characterize the aesthetic of the entire settlement; BELOW: Structural section through a typical house.

154

GENERATING NEW ARCHITECTURAL LANGUAGES

Stone Building System

Dar'a Province, Syria

Demir Holiday Village

Bodrum, Turkey

Panafrican Institute for Development

Ouagadougou, Burkina Faso

Entrepreneurship Development Institute of India

Ahmedabad, India

OPPOSITE: Demir Holiday Village, Bodrum, Turkey.

STONE BUILDING SYSTEM
DAR'A PROVINCE, SYRIA

Architects: Raif Muhanna, Ziad Muhanna, and Rafi Muhanna (civil engineer)

Client: The Ministry of Education

Completed: 1990 and ongoing

The rich cultural heritage of Syria has been extensively ignored in the architecture of the recent past where modern concepts and techniques are fashionable. In the face of this, the three Muhanna brothers - two architects and an engineer - proposed a new and challenging approach. With the help of computer technology and employing the arch and vault forms traditional to Syria, they designed a sophisticated building system that is specifically responsive to the local basalt. This combination of traditional ideas with modern technology has enormous possibilities for the future.

The Muhanna brothers successfully proved that their stone building system worked by using this technique to build their own house in Bassir. The system was officially patented in March 1988. The Prime Minister of Syria was so enthused by this new method that it was decided to commission a number of schools with the stone building system. The first four schools, all located in Dar'a province where basalt is plentiful, were completed in 1990.

The programme for the first completed school at Shagrawieh consists of six classrooms, one exterior hall, and two administration rooms. Each classroom is covered with a vaulted span of five metres. They are arranged in groups of two, and connected by an open, vaulted passageway. Vaults have demonstrably superior thermal characteristics, allowing hot air to rise and exit. As a portion of the outside vault surfaces always face away from the sun, this helps to further reduce the temperature inside the classrooms.

Building costs are low since the materials are available on the site - the maximum radius for gathering stones has been restricted to 15 kilometres. In fact, the cost of these schools is about one-third less than that of normal school buildings which use cement blocks and reinforced concrete structures.

It is clear that this project is very original in the contemporary context of Syria where architectural production is generally collective and anonymous. It challenges contemporary habits and presents a new way of embracing and connecting traditional forms

In addition to being easy to build, barrel vaults are environmentally sensible, since they channel breezes into the interior of the classrooms. A simple construction system, combined with basalt that is readily available in the area, add up to a prototype that is easily replicable.

with sophisticated design techniques. The building system invented by the Muhanna brothers can be applied to other rural constructions in any region where stone is available. Its potential is enormous.

The citation of the Jury reads:

The cultural meaning of this project is based on a deep understanding of rural reality by the architects. It challenges contemporary habits and construction trends. In a region where current schools reproduce anonymous, dull and alienating buildings, the use of vaulted spaces has created a challenging and original alternative. The architects chose to use local materials and local typology: basalt stone and vault construction. This technique was readily adapted by unskilled local labour and resulted in buildings that could be completed at a cost saving of one-third when compared to prevailing construction methods. The resultant structures are proud, memorable backdrops for the education of young Syrian boys and girls. Far from offering an archaic image, the elementary school offers a strong design, a wise plan, and a rational product which can be applied to all other types of rural construction where stone is available.

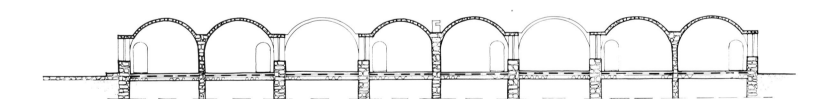

ABOVE: Longitudinal section showing the six classrooms and covered corridors; OPPOSITE: Each of the six classrooms in the school is covered with a vault that spans approximately 5 metres.

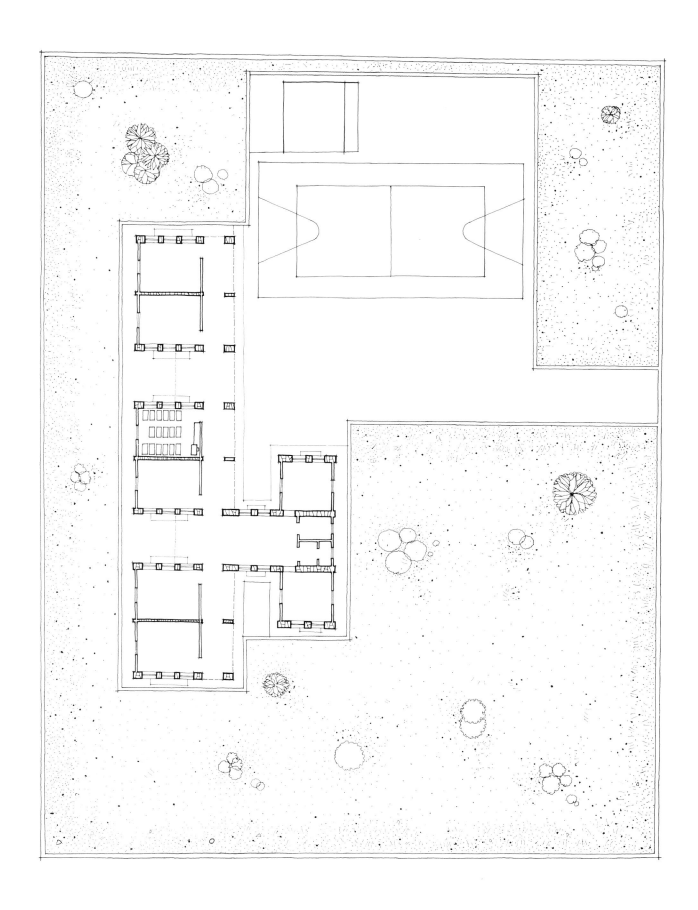

The Elementary School at As Suwayda' represents a rational approach to a clearly stated structural problem, which has been solved with elegant simplicity; ABOVE: Plan of the School.

DEMIR HOLIDAY VILLAGE
BODRUM, TURKEY

Architects: Turgut Cansever, Emine Ögün, Mehmet Ögün, and Feyza Cansever

Client: Tuyako A.S.

Completed: 1987 and ongoing

The Demir Holiday Village consists of thirty-five detached villas on a 50-hectare site which is located nine kilometres north of Bodrum. They are vacation houses for middle-class Turkish families, custom-designed for their occupants and beautifully executed. The villas form the first phase of a much larger development scheme which has yet to be realized.

The spectacular site is situated on a bay surrounded by national forest lands. It was bought many years ago by the architect, Turgut Cansever, and his partner, Tugrul Akçura, who established a company to develop it.

The architect, who is designer and developer as well as the executor of the project, devised unusual and ideal solutions for the execution of his scheme. In acquiring a large tract of land which was surrounded by reserve forests and the sea, he established his first objective, which was to create a vacation village that was not surrounded by poorly designed and built developments which have mushroomed all over that region. By limiting his basic construction materials to those that were available locally, he achieved his second objective of making a relevant and modern contribution to the architectural heritage of the area, a heritage with Greek, Byzantine and Ottoman layers. By selling the villas at a relatively high price, the architect ensured that the property would be well maintained. By offering a range of twelve villa types, he was able to custom-design houses for his clients, thereby making it commercially viable and architecturally varied.

Uniting all these ideas was the architect's paramount concern for protecting the environment and the amenity of the site. To this end, he defined a policy of conserving the trees and the soil: no trees could be cut and no soil was to be moved or brought in; cars were to be excluded as much as possible from the site; the shoreline was protected, and sea pollution was tightly controlled.

The architectural style was also designed to be harmonious with the cultural and natural surroundings. A common architectural language was evolved for the entire construction consisting of stone, wood,

An intentionally limited palette of materials as well as careful preservation of the landscape has ensured that the villas are compatible with their natural context.

165

and exposed concrete. Nine villa types have been constructed thus far. Each client was shown the 2.7 hectare site on which the villas were to be built. Within that area, future owners were free to choose any location for the site of their summer villas, and the only constraint was that a new house could not obstruct the sea views of a neighbour's. The sites were not laid out on a grid; plots were standard in area but not in shape. A wide range of stone wall textures and colours for shutters and doors adds further variety. The paths and lanes between the villas, the richly landscaped gardens and terraces, and the highly diverse yet controlled massing of the villas themselves create the look and feel of a natural settlement.

The wonder of these villas is the architect's skill at achieving almost an infinity of variation within the limits of a tightly restricted formal language.

Jury citation:

The Award is given for the foresight of the architect who has re-designed the traditional forms of local architecture to yield a coherent union of new and old materials. The result is refined yet simple. The well-crafted, beautifully sited houses set a high standard for architectural design, craftsmanship and commercial land development. A rich vocabulary of patterned stone walls and walkways and the sensitive integration of native plant materials create a seductive and peaceful retreat for the inhabitants. The careful layout of the modest, individual buildings retains the scenic view and preserves the landscape. The integral design of the restrained interiors is the product of an assured hand.

ABOVE: Roofs have been designed as decks to take advantage of an excellent climate and good views; OPPOSITE : Loadbearing stone walls, 50 cm. thick, are the primary structural and aesthetic language of the villa complex, which allowed local masons to work with a material familiar to them, as well as providing good thermal performance.

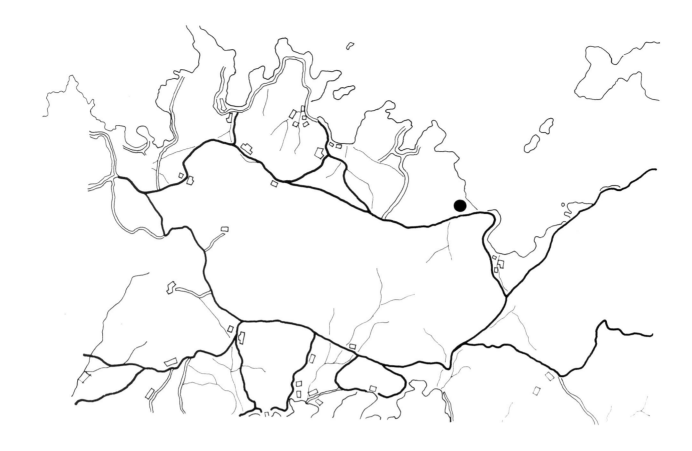

ABOVE: Overall plan of the Bodrum peninsula, with Demir shown as a black dot in the upper right, near the coast; BELOW: Master plan of the entire resort complex, with the existing houses shown on the upper right, near the coast; OPPOSITE: Each villa has been treated as an entity and yet has been sited in such a way as to contribute to the entire composition.

171

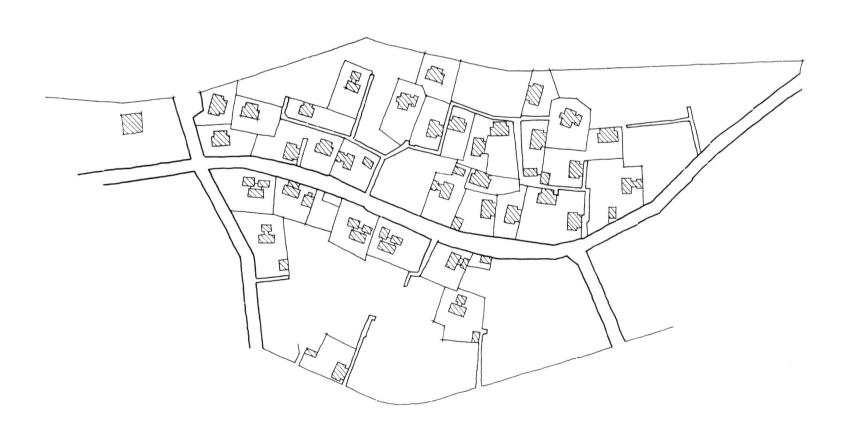

ABOVE:While details have been kept to a minimum, they have also been executed with great care; BELOW:Plan of phase one; OPPOSITE: The vernacular architecture of this region consists of simple repetitive modular units of local stone, punctuated with small rectangular windows. These can be seen all along the Aegean coast, and served as a model for the Demir villas.

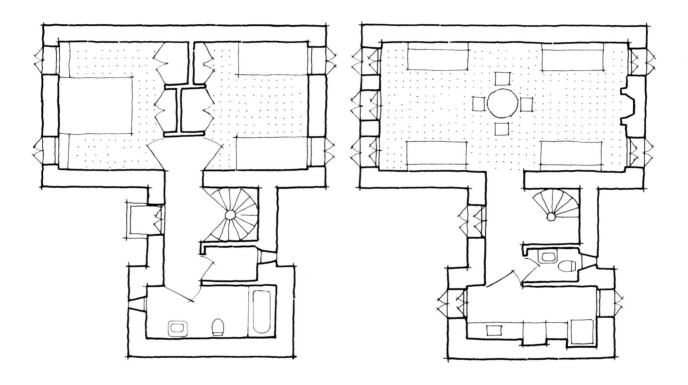

ABOVE: As with exterior details, interiors have been kept simple, but have been executed with painstaking care; BELOW: Plan of one of the nine villa types available: Type II D, gross area, 105 square metres; OPPOSITE: Labour intensive masonry techniques eventually evolved into a system of shuttering to control the accuracy of the walls and details, which reduced costs and shortened construction time.

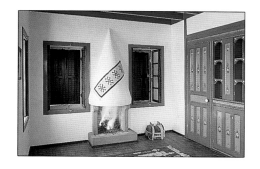

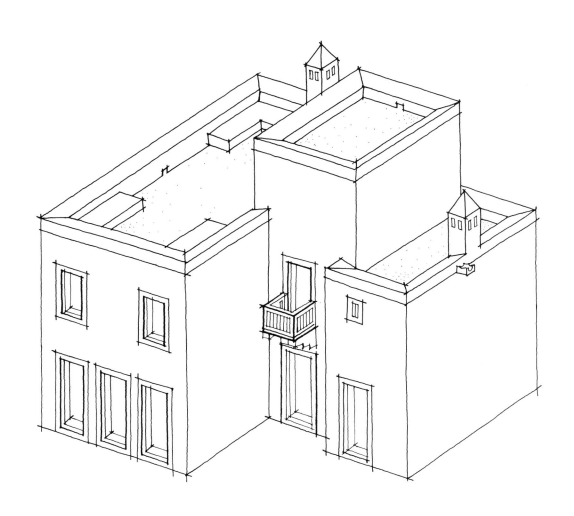

BELOW: Axonometric of Villa Type II D.

PANAFRICAN INSTITUTE FOR DEVELOPMENT
OUAGADOUGOU, BURKINA FASO

Architects: A.D.A.U.A. Burkina Faso
Jak Vauthrin, former Secretary General
Ladji Camara, Project Director and
Engineer
Philippe Glauser, Architect

Client: Panafrican Institute for Development
Malick Fall, Director
Faya Kondiano, Administration

Completed: 1984

From the early 1970s, it became increasingly clear that the African continent would be unable to resolve its development problems by simply adopting Western models. It was necessary to invent new models that would be better adapted to local resources and conditions. In 1978, the Panafrican Institute for Development commissioned the *Association pour le développement d'une architecture et d'un urbanisme africains* (ADAUA) to design and build the future campus of the Panafrican Institute for Development in the Sahel, at Ouagadougou. This project was entirely realized in stabilized earth brick. It aimed to demonstrate the creative potential of local materials and their appropriateness to the social and cultural context as well as to the climate of the Sahel region.

The objectives of this project were threefold: firstly, to design a viable type of construction using local materials; secondly, to make maximum use of local resources, both in material and labour, thereby reducing costs and foreign imports; and finally, by choosing to use traditional building techniques which require intensive labour, to create many jobs, and train masons and brick-makers. In the long term, this could lead to the creation of co-operatives that would help disseminate these objectives and these building techniques.

The campus of the Institute, built on a six-hectare plot given by the government, includes a teaching and administrative centre with an attached library and restaurant, housing for seventy-two students, and nine detached villas for the professors. These structures form a dense, urban-like fabric. Most of the buildings are designed on an introverted plan, and covered

spaces are generally grouped around courtyards. The courtyards come in various sizes; they are planted and shaded, and give a sense of privacy, natural ventilation, and coolness. The warm orange and yellow colours of the walls add a vibrant dimension.

The Institute was built entirely of stabilized earth bricks. The earth was procured from land some 3 kilometres away, and the cement used for the stabilization (the only import) came from Togo. The vaulted and domed roofs, also built of stabilized bricks, were mounted by the masons without the use of shuttering and show daring and virtuosity.

This stabilized earth brick technology, developed by the ADAUA, achieved spectacular results by setting rigorous standards. The Panafrican Institute for Development demonstrates a precision that is unusual in earth construction. Its crisp silhouettes and shaded spaces make a sophisticated statement that fits the hard light of the Sahel.

In the words of the Jury's citation:
This project demonstrates the creative potential of local materials and their appropriateness to the socio-cultural context and the climatic constraints of the Sahel region. The Institute represents one of the most impressive contemporary realizations in stabilized mud brick in Africa. It is a modern work that makes use of improved, inexpensive materials and intermediate building technologies, a good example of architectural ingenuity and technical virtuosity. The architectural environment, inspired by the work of Hassan Fathy, is created by a complex variety of rich, vault and dome forms, and the interior courtyards and verandas temper the harsh climate. The design is inspired by the organization of space in Volta villages. Brick patterns and graphic art enliven and unify the complex. The Institute embodies integrated development, community training and technical mastery.

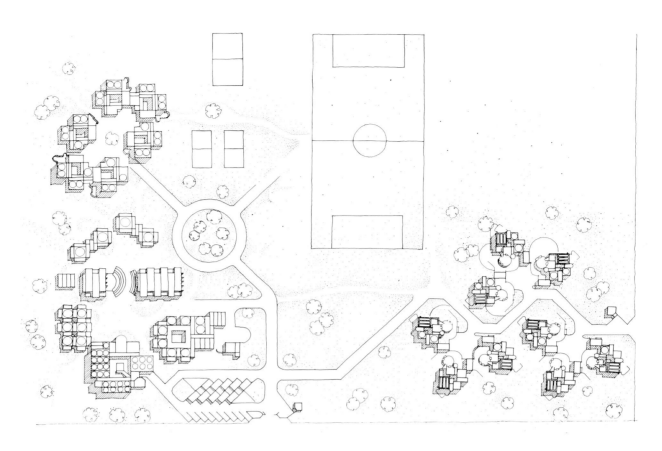

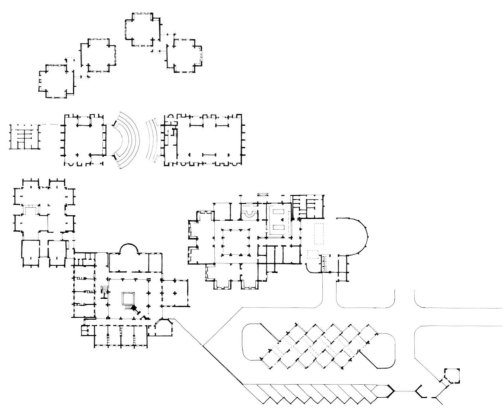

ABOVE: General site plan showing,clockwise from top left, student housing, professors' housing, and teaching and administrative centre; BELOW: Plan of administration building, classrooms and restaurant.

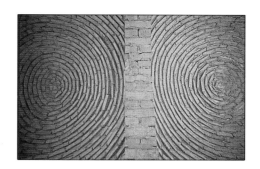

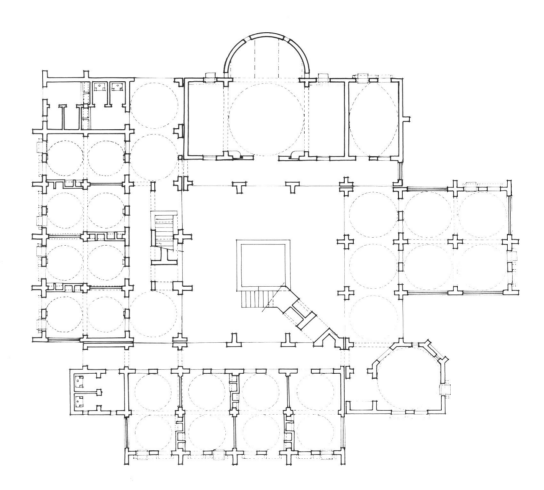

The architectural forms of the Institute, while generically derived from the Nubian vault and dome system popularized by Hassan Fathy, are specifically influenced by the playful, vernacular structures in the Upper Volta region, which have colourful graphic patterns inscribed on their façades; BELOW: Plan of the administration building, with offices organized around an open central court.

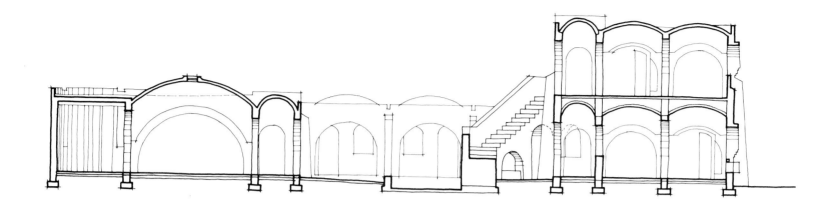

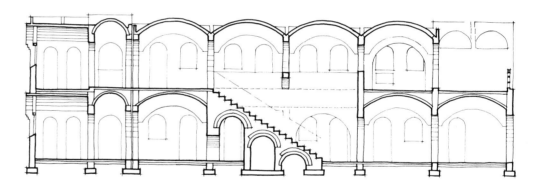

In describing this project, Jak Vauthrin, the founder of the ADAUA, has said, "we used our imagination and powers of invention to set up the first small industries for producing bricks from earth to show that the local lateritic soil contains all that is needed to build any building required"; ABOVE AND BELOW: Sections through administration building.

ENTREPRENEURSHIP DEVELOP-MENT INSTITUTE OF INDIA
AHMEDABAD, INDIA

Architect: Bimal Hasmukh C. Patel

Client: Entrepreneurship Development Institute of India
Viharibhai G. Patel, Director

Contractors: Ganon Dunkerly and Company

Completed: 1987

The revolutionary concept of training entrepreneurs was pioneered in Ahmedabad in 1969. The idea developed and gradually became a national movement. Every state wanted to develop its own programme, resulting in the need for a national institution for entrepreneurship, one that would supervise all the others. Thus, the Entrepreneurship Development Institute of India (EDII) was established in 1983. A national competition with an innovative brief for the design of the EDII was elaborated in 1985. It was won by the young architect, Bimal Patel.

The Institute is composed of seven buildings organized on two axes. Along one axis are two hostels, a kitchen and a dining hall. The other axis is shared by the remaining four buildings: the administrative centre, the training and research centres, and the library. An auditorium was designed but has not yet been built.

The Institute responds well to the users' needs. The skilful grouping of two-storeyed buildings around open spaces, each with a distinct function and character yet linked to the two main axes, provides coherence for the various activities. Open arcades are used to organize the entire complex as well as the individual buildings, taking the best advantage of the pleasant surroundings and courtyards.

The courtyards were landscaped with stone pavements and grass and shaded by batam trees specially chosen for the large size of their leaves. The area around the buildings was also landscaped and planted with a grid of trees. In a few years, these trees will create a forest-like atmosphere.

Climatic control has been one of the major design concerns. The area of the courtyards is large in proportion to the building heights, and this keeps the buildings well ventilated. Galleries around the courtyards create a transition space between the harsh light

ABOVE: Because of the shading tactics used by the architect, classroom interiors stay cool most of the year without costly mechanical equipment.

189

of the court and the shaded rooms inside the buildings. The windows are recessed and protected against
monsoon rains. The need for costly heating or cooling
has been virually eliminated. According to the users,
the inside room temperatures are comfortable for the
major part of the year.

Construction materials were chosen by the architect
to conform to the restricted budget. Brick and concrete
are the basic materials used, and both are locally
available. Exposed concrete is used to accentuate the
lintels over windows and doors as well as the arches
which span the circulation corridors.

The buildings of the Entrepreneurship Development
Institute are simple, handsome and contemporary. This
young architect should be proud of his achievement.

The Jury's citation of this project reads as fol-
lows:

*This innovative programme in education and training
in entrepreneurship is housed in an open, congenial
campus. The fruitful collaboration between the
director of the Institute and the architect produced a
fine example of a low-cost, low-maintenance building
which promises easy replicability. The architect is
commended for his confident use of formal elements
growing out of the Indo-Islamic architectural heritage.
A series of geometrically structured courtyards and
loggias are the primary organizing framework. The
variation of open, closed and transitional spaces
provides light and shade, and creates an inviting
environment for work, interaction and repose.*

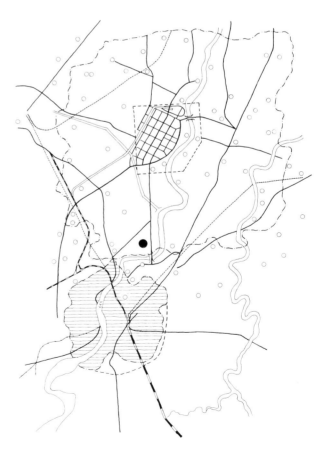

*The complex responds well to the client's needs because of
the skilful positioning of buildings and open spaces; BELOW:
Location of the Entrepreneurship Development Institute on
the outskirts of Ahmedabad.*

194

ABOVE: Classrooms are functional and comfortable;
BELOW: Site plan of the EDII campus; OPPOSITE ABOVE
AND BELOW: The main open quadrangle in the centre of
the Institute and a subsidiary courtyard grouping.

195

1917, the Uzbek Soviet Socialist Republic was formed with Samarkand as its capital from 1924 to 1930. Subsequently the capital shifted to Tashkent and Samarkand became the second most important administrative centre of Uzbekistan. Samarkand today is the second largest city in Uzbekistan and remains an industrial and cultural centre.

It has a large university and important institutes specializing in teaching, architecture, medicine, agriculture, scientific research and sheep breeding. The town also has major theatres for opera, ballet and variety performances. There is an important museum of history, culture and the art of Central Asia located in the town. As in the past, Samarkand continues to export dried fruit, cotton, rice, and leather to other parts of the world.

Uzbekistan, situated in the heart of Central Asia, is located between the Amu Darya and Syr Darya Rivers, the Aral Sea and the Tien Shan mountains. In its north-western half, Uzbekistan is largely a desert, while its southern half includes the fertile valleys of the river systems of Ferghana and Zerafshan that were the lifelines for the ancient cities of Bukhara, Ferghana and Samarkand. The Uzbeks take their name from a 14th century ruler named Khan Uzbek, and have their origins in the Turko-Mongol tribes who were once nomadic pastoralists. Today, the city of Samarkand is multinational and its population of 390,000, as of 1989, comprises ninety nationalities. According to recent data, the region has a population of 20 million which includes Uzbeks (68%), Russians (11%), Tantras, Kazakhs and Tajiks (each 4%), Kara-Kalpaks (2%), and Korlans (1%). In the last twenty years, the population of the city of Samarkand has increased by 110,000. Due to recent institutional changes, many Russians are now leaving the area.

The wealth of the region around Samarkand comes both from its agricultural fertility as well as its industrial might. During the period from 1981 to 1985, something like 17,000 hectares of new land was brought under irrigated cultivation. There are many large farms specializing in poultry and cattle breeding in the region. Apart from supplying raw cotton, the region around Samarkand produces the highest amount of dried fruit, tobacco, raisins, grapes and meat in Uzbekistan. It is also the second largest producer of vegetables, fresh fruit, milk and Karakul pelts.

Samarkand, which now covers over 15,000 hectares, is also an important railway junction of the Krasnovodsk-Tashkent line and its airport is the second largest in Uzbekistan after Tashkent.

The pre-modern city of Samarkand has been the subject of a number of plans that have aimed at giving a formal direction to its expansion and modernisation. The basic approach taken by previous town planners has been to consider the modern and the pre-modern settlements as one unit and to find ways of integrating them. The planning of green avenues passing through the town has been considered to be one way to attempt this integration. The Russian planners, in the last century, had located their extension of the city along the curved avenues towards the west of the old town to encircle the site of the citadel. At that time, the clearing of the remains of Timur's citadel and the location of the military camp on the site had provided the only meeting point between the old pre-modern Timurid settlement and the new Russian colonial settlement. Subsequently, the political and administrative centre was built during the Soviet period where the military camp was once located.

The territory of the citadel site, and the area between it and the Registan complex has therefore remained the symbolic centre of Samarkand from Timur's time to today. During the Timurid and post-Timurid period, the network of narrow streets and passages that linked the gates in the city walls all converged in the area of what is known today as the Registan square. Plans drawn up in the 1890s laid down a broad tree-lined avenue running north-east to south-west that connected the new settlement to the citadel. This avenue remains a focal spine for the masterplan drawn up in 1981, which shows a major expansion of the town along this spine towards the south-west of the city.[20]

Today Islam is once again practised freely in the Ferghana Valley, and the construction of mosques and madrasas has continued, making it possible for the architectural traditions of the past, which are so responsible for the individual character of Samarkand, to be re-established once again.   *JS*

Notes

1. W. Barthold, *Turkestan Down to the Mongol Invasion*, C.E. Bosworth, London, 1968, p.181

2. Ibid., p.182

3. Ibid., p.182

4. J. Schacht and C.E. Bosworth, *The Legacy of Islam*, Oxford at the Clarendon Press, 1974, p. 118 (see also W. Barthold, op. cit., p. 183)

5. J. Schacht and C.E. Bosworth, op. cit., p.117

6. Ibid., p.120

7. W. Barthold, op. cit., p.189

8. Ibid., p.189

9. J. Schacht and C.E. Bosworth, op. cit., p.117

10. W. Barthold, op. cit., p. 237

11. Ibid., p. 196

12. Ibid., p. 210

13. Ibid., p. 213

14. Ibid., p. 287

15. E.G. Brown, *The Chahar Magala of Nidhami-i-Arudi-Samarqandi*, trans. Hertford, 1899, pp. 75-77

16. W. Barthold, op. cit., p. 322

17. Lisa Golombek and Donald Wilber, *The Timurid Architecture of Iran and Turan*, Princeton University Press, 1988, p. 3

18. Ibid., p. 4

19. *Samarkand Revitalisation*, Competition Brochure by the Aga Khan Trust for Culture, 1991, pp. 23-26

20. Ibid. This description of Timurid monuments and contemporary Samarkand is based on information in the Competition Brochure.

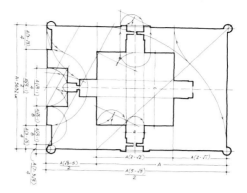

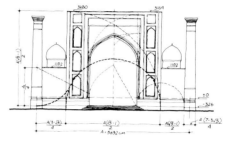

ABOVE: Typical plan, showing geometric ratios; Mathematical relationships of a typical elevation; PREVIOUS PAGE: Interior View of the Tillya Kari Madrasa and Mosque.

PROJECT DATA

KAIROUAN CONSERVATION PROGRAMME, Kairouan, Tunisia

Personnel
Client: The Municipality of Kairouan.
Conservators and Planners: Association de Sauvegarde de la Médina de Kairouan (ASM), Brahmin Chabbouh, President, former Conservator of the *Medina* of Kairouan; Mourad Rammah, Secretary General, and Conservator of the *Medina* of Kairouan; Hedi Ben Lahmar, Architect for Historical Monuments; Hassen Jelliti, Project Manager; Abdelaziz Trabelsi, Project Manager; Ahmed Gdah, Photographer, Abdellatif Guilene, Draughtsman

Timetable
Inception: Creation of ASM, 1977
Construction: Restoration Phase 1: 1977-1992
Occupancy: ongoing
Restoration: Ibn Khayrun (Three Door Mosque), Khan Barrouta, Mosque of Al Bey, Bir Barrouta, Mausoleum of Sidi Khedidi, Mausoleum of Sidi Abid al Ghariani, Mausoleum of Sidi Abada, Mausoleum of Sidi Sahib, Suq of Cisterns, the Water Basins of the Aghlabids, and the Ramparts of the *Medina*

PALACE PARKS PROGRAMME, Istanbul, Turkey

Personnel
Client: The Turkish Grand National Assembly
Conservators and Architects: Staff of the Regional Offices of the National Palaces Trust (NPT), Metin Sözen, Director.
Consultants: Sazi Sirel, Lighting; Erol Eti, Önder Küçükerman, Murat Eric, Can Apak, and Sise Cam, Porcelain and Stained Glass; Muzaffer Özkaya, Mustafa Bayram, Abdi Dalfes, Turgut Tüfekçi, and Isa Ilisu, Interior Lighting and Security; Alaattin Yavasca, Necdet Yasar, Bekir Sitki Sezgin, Ihsan Özgen, and Haydar Sanal, Musical Research; Ugur Erkman, Necati Inceoglu, Mine Inceoglu, Stable; Sami Sekeroglu, Cem Odman, and Alp Birol, Promotional Films and Documentaries; Adnan Cakiroglu, Ismet Aka, Müfit Yorulmaz and Ergün Togrol, Structure; Hakki Yildiz, Mübahat Kütükoglu, Mücteba Ilgürel, Münir Aktepe, Filiz Cagman, and Zarif Orgun. Archival Research; Muammer Ülker, Calligraphy and Inscriptions; Yüksel Özoguz, Nuran Kutlu, and Jale Parla, Languages; Erdal Aksoy, Photography; Sema Germaner and Zeynep Inankur, Paintings; Mustafa Cezar and Filiz Cagman, Editors; Cengiz Yildizci, Landscape Design; Ümit Serdaroglu, Restoration; Süha Toner, Repairs; Gündüz Gökçe, Muhtesem Giray and Belkis Mutlu, Restoration; Mümtaz Isingör, Ilban Öz and Gülay Bakircioglu, Exhibitions

Timetable
Inception: Creation of NPT 1983. *Conservation Seminars,* 1984.
Construction and Occupancy: 1984 and ongoing. Dolmabahçe Palace (1984-1989), Beylerbeyi Palace (1984-1989), Aynalikavak Pavilion (1985-1989), Maslak Lodges (1986), Ihlamur (1985), and Yildiz Sale (1985-1990)

CULTURAL PARK FOR CHILDREN, Cairo, Egypt

Personnel
Client: The Ministry of Culture, Farouk Hosny, Minister; the late Abd al-Hamid Radwan, former Minister.
Architect: Caravan Community Design Collaborative, Abdelhalim Ibrahim Abdelhalim, principal, and project team: N. Ammar, A. Behairy, H. Saker, A. Saloom. M. Sharkawy, R. Dahan, E.Mostafa, H. Abou Zeid, H. Zaini, R. Farag.*Contractor:* El Giza General Contracting Company, Fathy El-Nessr, Chairman.*Site Supervision:* M. Abdel-Razik, A. Behairy, M. Nour, A. Labib, Nagat Sanyoor, Y. Shaa-er. *Master Craftsmen:* M. Ashour, M. Eibeda, M. Fathy, A. Khamis, and S. Bahr
Community: A. Abdelwehab, local district chairman, M. Abdel Moneam, Abu al-Dahab Street Council

Timetable
Inception: Competition, June 1983.
Construction: January 1987 to October 1989

EAST WAHDAT UPGRADING PROGRAMME, Amman, Jordan

Personnel
Client: Government of Jordan, Urban Development Department (UDD)
Feasibility: Jouzy and Partners with Halcrow Fox Associates, David Walton, Project Director; Roy Brockman, Economist; Rifaat Darghouth, Architect; Elie Halaby, Engineer; Salah Hariri, Architect; David Jordan, Sociologist
Specialist Advice: Mohammed Barhoum, Sociology; Roger England, Health Planning; Najeeb Tleel, Public Health Engineering; Mick Yaxley, Slum Upgrading
UDD Staff: Yousef Hiasat, Director; Hisham D. Zagha, Director from 1980-1990; Khalid Jayyousi and Majid Nabir, Design and Layout; Jemal Al Dali and Sawsan Daibas, Social Surveys; Rita Mansour and Nashwa Subh, House Designs; Usama Rabeeh, Civil Engineering; Sahar Al Majali, Finance; Eman E. Riyal, Marketing; Leila Bisharat, Magdy Tewfik, Steney Shami and Lucine Taminian, Surveys; Hidaya Khairi, Population Affairs; Jamal Ibrahim Al-Dali, Community Development; Marah Jamal Al-Khayyat and Monah Batayneh, Studies; and Ghaleb Khalil Al-Azzeh, Social Research.
Contractor: China State Construction and local enterprises

Timetable
Feasibility: 1978. *Inception:* 1980. *Establish Tenure:* 1981 onwards. *Infrastructure and Site Services:* 1982-1984. *Private House Building:* 1982 and ongoing. *Occupancy:* 1982 and ongoing

KAMPUNG KALI CHO-DE, Yogyakarta, Indonesia

Personnel
Community: Koperasi Permukiman dan Lingkungan Hidcup Code Gondolayu, the residents' co-operative
Architect: Yousef B. Mangunwijaya *Advisor:* Willi Prasetya
Consultants: Lembaga Pengabdian Masyarakat; Duta Wacana University; and Yayasan Pondok Rakyat, People's Housing Foundation
Artists: Volunteer Art Students in Yogyakarta
Builders: Prawiro and Comrades, village craftsmen and slum dwellers

Timetable
Inception: 1983. *Construction:* 1983-1985

STONE BUILDING SYSTEM, Dar'a Province, Syria

Personnel
Client: The Ministry of Education
Architects: Raif Muhanna, Ziad Muhanna, and Rafi Muhanna, Civil Engineer
Contractors: General Company for Engineering and Consulting

Timetable
Inception: 1987. Patent: 1988. *Construction* of four schools: Shagrawieh, Konetrau, Dar'a and Deir Ali: 1990

DEMIR HOLIDAY VILLAGE, Bodrum, Turkey

Personnel
Client: Turistik Yatrimlar Adi Komandit Sti. (TUYAKO A.S.)
Architects: Turgut Cansever, Principal Designer; Emine Ögün, Site Planning and Unit Planning; Mehmet Ögün, Construction, Details and Garden Design; and Feyza Cansever, Unit Design
Consultants: Niyazi Parlar, Structure; Pertev Erdi, Electrical; Müjdat Sayin, Sanitary and Mechanical; Necati Celik, Clerk-of-Works

Timetable
Inception: creation of TUYAKO A.S. 1971. *Design Development:* 1971-1983 (due to protracted negotiations with the Ministry of Forestry). *Construction:* 1983-1990. Occupancy: 1985

PANAFRICAN INSTITUTE FOR DEVELOPMENT, Ouagadougou, Burkina Faso

Personnel
Client: Panafrican Institute for Development: Fernand Vincent, Secretary General 1963-1980; Ibrahim Diallo, Director IPD/AOS (1978-1990); Malick Fall, Director IPD/AOS (since 1990); Faya Kondiano, Administration
Architects: Association pour le Developpement Naturel d'une Architecture et d'un Urbanisme Africains (ADAUA): Jak Vauthrin, founder and former Secretary General; Ladji Camara, Project Director and Engineer; Philippe Glauser, Architect; Gérard Woba, Djibril Diagne, Daniel Kadsondo, and Y. Belemnaba, Project Team
Master Craftsmen: ADAUA-trained masons and bricklayers with local enterprises

Timetable
Inception: 1978. Finance: 1980. *Construction:* 1982-1984

ENTREPRENEURSHIP DEVELOPMENT INSTITUTE OF INDIA, Ahmedabad, India

Personnel
Client: Entrepreneurship Development Institute of India: Viharibhai G. Patel, Director
Architect: Hasmukh C. Patel, Architects and Planners; Bimal Hasmukh C Patel, Design Partner; J.M. Gunjaria, Architect; A.I. Patel, Engineer; and Arvind Patel, Engineer
Consultants: Vakil-Mehta-Sheth Consulting Engineers, Structure; S.K. Murthy Consulting Engineers, Electrical and Sanitary Installations; P.B. Bhagyat, Landscape
Contractor: Ganon Dunkerly and Company

Timetable
Design: 1985-1987. *Construction:* 1986-1987.
Occupancy: June 1987